KU-285-220

The **AA** **POCKET**Guide

SCOTLAND

Original text by Hugh Taylor and Moira McCrossan
Updated by Robin Barton

© Automobile Association Developments Limited 2008. First published 2008

ISBN: 978-0-7495-5532-0

Published by AA Publishing, a trading name of Automobile Association Developments Limited, whose registered office is Fanum House, Basing View, Basingstoke, Hampshire RG21 4EA. Registered number 1878835.

Colour separation: Keenes, Andover
Printed and bound in Italy by Printer Trento S.r.l.

Front cover images: (t) AA/J Carnie; (b) AA/J Smith
Back cover image: AA/S L Day

About this book

Symbols are used to denote the following categories:

✚ map reference

✉ address or location

☎ telephone number

◷ opening times

✋ admission charge

🍴 restaurant or café on premises or nearby

Ⓜ nearest underground train station

🚌 nearest bus/tram route

Ⓡ nearest overground train station

⛴ nearest ferry stop

✈ nearest airport

❓ other practical information

ℹ tourist information office

➤ indicates the page where you will find a fuller description

This book is divided into four sections.

Planning pages 6–19
Before you go; Getting there; Getting around; Being there

Best places to see pages 20–41
The unmissable highlights of any visit to Scotland

Exploring pages 42–125
The best places to visit in Scotland organized by area

Maps pages 129–144
All map references are to the atlas section. For example, Inveraray has the page number and reference ✚ 130 A4 – indicating the grid square in which it can be found

Contents

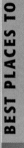

Planning

Before you go

WHEN TO GO

JAN	FEB	MAR	APR	MAY	JUN	JUL	AUG	SEP	OCT	NOV	DEC
5°C	5°C	8°C	11°C	14°C	16°C	18°C	18°C	15°C	11°C	9°C	7°C
41°F	41°F	46°F	52°F	57°F	61°F	64°F	64°F	59°F	52°F	48°F	45°F

🔵 High season   🔵 Low season

With the North Sea on three sides, Scotland's climate is nothing if not unpredictable. Seasonal variations in temperature and rainfall differ regionally. The highlands of the Cairngorms can suffer blizzards in late spring while areas of the west coast, warmed by the Gulf Stream, can be mild enough for tropical plants. Late spring (May–Jun) tends to be drier than the middle of the summer (Jul–Aug) and the east coast tends to have less rainfall than the west. Temperatures are variable, but July and August are usually the hottest months with average temperatures of up to 20°C (68°F). One seasonal feature to consider is the hatching of the midges, tiny biting insects prevalent in some rural areas. The midges appear in June and don't die out until the cooler weather of September. The west of Scotland suffers greater midge outbreaks than the east.

WHAT YOU NEED

		UK	Germany	USA	Netherlands	Spain
●	Required					
○	Suggested					
▲	Not required	Some countries require a passport to remain valid for a minimum period (usually at least six months) beyond the date of entry – check before you travel.				
Passport		▲	●	●	●	●
Visa (Regulations can change—check before booking your journey)		▲	▲	▲	▲	▲
Onward or Return Ticket		▲	○	○	○	○
Health Inoculations		▲	▲	▲	▲	▲
Health Documentation (➤ 9, Health Insurance)		▲	●	●	●	▲
Travel Insurance		○	○	○	○	○
Driving Licence (national)		●	●	●	●	●
Car Insurance Certificate (if own car)		▲	●	●	●	●
Car Registration Document (if own car)		▲	●	●	●	●

WEBSITES

www.visithighlands.com
www.edinburgh.org

www.seeglasgow.com
www.scot-borders.co.uk

TOURIST OFFICES AT HOME

In Scotland

Scottish Tourist Board
23 Ravelston Terrace,
Edinburgh EH4 3TP
☎ 0131 332 2433
www.visitscotland.com

In the USA

British Tourist Authority
551 Fifth Avenue,
7th Floor, Suite 701,
New York, NY 10176-0799
☎ 800/462 2748

In England

Scottish Tourist Board
19 Cockspur Street
London SW1 5BL
☎ 020 7930 2812

HEALTH INSURANCE

Nationals of the EU and certain other countries receive reduced cost emergency medical treatment in the UK with the relevant documentation, although private medical insurance is still advised and is essential for all other visitors.

Dental treatment is very limited under the National Health Service scheme and even EU nationals will probably have to pay. However, private medical insurance will cover you.

TIME DIFFERENCES

GMT
12 noon

Scotland
12 noon

Germany
1PM

USA (NY)
7AM

Netherlands
1PM

Spain
1PM

Scottish time, like the rest of the UK, is on Greenwich Mean Time. The clocks are advanced by one hour in the spring and brought back one hour in the autumn. Continental Europe is always at least one hour ahead.

NATIONAL HOLIDAYS

Scottish public holidays may vary from place to place and their dates from year to year, so although the capital Edinburgh may be on holiday at certain times, other Scottish towns and cities will not necessarily be having a public holiday. Major holidays throughout the country are:

1 Jan *New Year's Day*
2 Jan *Bank Holiday*
Mar/Apr *Good Friday/Easter Monday*
First Mon May *May Day Bank Holiday*
Last Mon May *Spring Bank Holiday*
Last Mon Aug *August Bank Holiday*
25 Dec *Christmas Day*
26 Dec *Boxing Day*

WHAT'S ON WHEN

January *The Ba',* Orkney: Very dangerous game of street soccer between two teams, the Uppies and the Downies, played through the streets of Kirkwall, seemingly with few rules.

Celtic Connections, Royal Concert Hall, Glasgow: Three weeks of music and culture.

Up Helly Aa, Lerwick, Shetland: Annual Viking Fire Festival which takes place on the last Tuesday in January irrespective of the weather.

Robert Burns Night: On the anniversary of the poet's birthday (25 January) people gather for a traditional Burns Supper of haggis, neeps and tatties, a few drams of whisky, and poetry and song.

February *Scottish Curling Championship:* Grown men and women hurl lumps of rock along ice.

March *Whuppity Stoorie,* Lanark: Winter is symbolically banished by children running round the church hitting each other with paper weapons.

April *The Scottish Grand National,* Ayr Racecourse.

Edinburgh International Folk Festival.

May *Girvan Traditional Folk Festival:* A picturesque fishing harbour, intimate concert venues with top performers and unbelievable pub sessions combine to make this the best small folk festival in Scotland.

May Day Bank Holiday: Long weekend.

Beltane Fire Festival, Calton Hill, Edinburgh: On 1 May, an ancient Pagan festival to celebrate the coming of spring.

June *Riding the Marches,* various Border towns: Traditionally to check the boundaries of the common land.

July *World Flounder Tramping Championships,* Palnackie, Dumfriesshire: When the little fish tickle your feet you realize this event is not as easy as it sounds.

Moniaive Gala: Picturesque Dumfriesshire village at its best. Procession followed by a fair, and in the evening a ceilidh dance.

August *Edinburgh Arts Festival, Fringe and Military Tattoo.*

September *Braemar Highland Games:* Games take place across Scotland, but this is the one to see.

October *The National Mod:* Gaeldom's competition showcase. A different Highland town is chosen as the venue each year.

30 November *St. Andrew's Day.*

31 December *Hogmanay:* Seeing the old year out and the new one in. Traditional first-footing – visiting neighbours and friends with a bottle and something to eat – is dying out. Instead, parties are the trend with Edinburgh's Princes Street Gardens the venue for the world's largest.

Getting there

BY AIR

Glasgow Airport		
🚆	N/A	
🚌	20 minutes	
🚗	15 minutes	

14 kilometres (9 miles) to city centre

Edinburgh Airport		
🚆	N/A minutes	
🚌	25 minutes	
🚗	25 minutes	

14 kilometres (9 miles) to city centre

Scotland has four main international airports – Glasgow, Edinburgh, Aberdeen and Prestwick. Scheduled and charter flights arrive daily at all of them from Europe, USA and the rest of the UK. There are direct flights to Glasgow from North America.

EDINBURGH

Edinburgh's airport (www.edinburghairport.com) is to the west of the city.

Public transport There is no rail link between the airport, to the west of the city centre on the ring road, and central Edinburgh. However, a public bus service, the Airlink 100, runs from the Arrivals exit at the airport to Waverley Bridge in central Edinburgh every 10 minutes from 4.45am to past midnight. Tickets cost £3 one-way and £5 round-trip and can be purchased in the Arrivals hall or on the bus (☎ 0131 555 6363; www.flybybus.com).

The Edinburgh Shuttle (☎ 0845 500 5000; www.edinburghtransport.co.uk) offers shared minibuses to destinations within the city centre (including hotels and private homes). The service departs every 15–30 minutes and costs £8 each way.

Taxi There are three taxi stands at the airport, with private hire vehicles operating from the east end of the terminal and black cabs departing from the coach park. The third rank is on the ground floor of the short-stay car park. Travel time into the city is about 25 minutes; allow longer during the rush hour. Many taxis are wheelchair accessible.

Car To drive from the airport to Edinburgh, take the eastbound A8, which leads to the centre. Alternatively, follow the A8 west until the M9 intersection; the M9 heads to Stirling while the M8 goes to Glasgow.

GLASGOW

Glasgow's airport (www.glasgowairport.com) is just off the M8 motorway.

Public transport The nearest rail station is Paisley's Gilmour Street station, 2km (1 mile) from the airport. A taxi will drop you at the station. From Gilmour Street there is a frequent service to Glasgow Central station (between 5 and 8 trains an hour). Buses for the city centre depart from the Departures exit. Citylink's 905 service goes from Bay 3 to Glasgow Central rail station (☎ 0870 550 5050; www.citylink.co.uk). The bus is wheelchair accessible. The trip, departing every 7–15 minutes daily from 5.40am until midnight (less frequently on Sunday) takes 25 minutes and costs £3.50 one-way and £5.30 round-trip.

Taxi and car There is a taxi stand outside the terminal building with taxis available 24 hours a day. Drivers should take the M8 motorway into the centre.

Getting around

PUBLIC TRANSPORT

Internal flights British Airways (☎ 0870 850 9850; www.firstgroup.com/scotrail) has scheduled flights linking the main cities and provides a service to the islands, including Orkney and Shetland.

Trains Most of Scotland's rail service is operated by First Scotrail (☎ 0845 601 5929). GNER (☎ 08457 225 225; www.gner.co.uk) and Virgin (☎ 08457 222333; www.virgintrains.co.uk) also operate services.

Long-distance buses Scottish Citylink (☎ 08705 505 050; www.citylink.co.uk) covers most of the country as well as linking to the rest of the UK. The buses are mostly modern and comfortable. Several local companies provide connecting services to areas not covered by Citylink and in the Highlands, Islands and remote rural areas there are Post Buses run by the Royal Mail (☎ 08457 740 740).

Ferries Caledonian MacBrayne (☎ 08705 650 000; www.calmac.co.uk) has an extensive service covering the main island destinations on the West Coast including the Western Islands. For Orkney and Shetland, Northlink Ferries (☎ 0845 600 0449) has regular sailings from Aberdeen.

Urban transport In the main towns and cities the public transport network is fairly extensive. Glasgow has Scotland's only underground and is also well served by urban trains and buses. Elsewhere a plethora of bus companies compete for passengers.

FARES AND TICKETS

Tickets are often cheaper if purchased in advance. Some forms of transport are more expensive at peak times; planes and trains especially so. Off-peak periods tend to start after 9.15am and include weekends.

TAXIS

In cities and larger towns the standard black hackney cabs are licensed, have meters and should display rates. Minicabs and private rental cars will also be licensed and may be metered. If not, agree on a fare before entering the vehicle.

DRIVING

- Speed limit on motorways and two-way highways 112kph (70mph).
- Speed limit on all other roads 96kph (60mph).
- Speed limits on urban roads 48kph (30mph).
- Seat belts must be worn in front and rear seats at all times.
- Random breath-testing. Never drive under the influence of alcohol.
- Fuel (petrol) is expensive and available in two grades: Unleaded and Super Unleaded, in addition to diesel. Prices vary and it is much more expensive in the Highlands and Islands. The least expensive fuel is sold at supermarkets with filling stations. Opening hours are variable with some 24-hour stations on motorways (highways) and large urban areas.
- SOS telephones are located at regular intervals along motorways (highways). Roadside assistance operated by the Automobile Association (☎ 0800 887 766; www.theaa.com) has a 24-hour breakdown service for members and for members of organizations with reciprocal agreements.

CAR RENTAL

Most major companies have facilities at airports, major towns and cities. Reserving in advance can avoid lengthy waits at peak periods. Avis (☎ 08700 100 287; www.avis.co.uk). Budget (☎ 0870 156 5656; www.budget.co.uk). Thrifty (☎ 01494 751 540; www.thrifty.co.uk).

Being there

TOURIST OFFICES

Edinburgh and Lothians
3 Princes Street (above Waverley
Station), Edinburgh
☎ 0131 473 3800
www.edinburgh.org

Greater Glasgow and the
Clyde Valley
11 George Square, Glasgow
☎ 0141 204 4480
www.seeglasgow.com

Dundee and Angus
21 Castle Street, Dundee
☎ 01382 527527
www.angusanddundee.co.uk

Aberdeen & Grampian
Exchange House
27 Albyn Place, Aberdeen
☎ 01224 288828
www.aberdeen-grampian.co.uk

Dumfries and Galloway
64 Whitesands, Dumfries
☎ 01387 245550
www.dumfriesandgalloway.co.uk

Shetland
Market Cross
Lerwick, Shetland
☎ 01595 693434
www.visitshetland.com

MONEY

The British unit of currency is the pound sterling, divided into 100p
(pence). Its symbol, placed before the pounds, is £. There are coins for
1 and 2p (copper), 5, 10, 20 and 50p (silver), £1 (gold-colour), £2 (silver and
gold-colour); and bank notes for 5, 10, 20, 50 and 100 pounds. Scotland,
unlike the rest of the UK, also has £1 banknotes. The pound is often
referred to as a quid; £5 is five quid or a fiver, while £10 is called a tenner.

TIPS/GRATUITIES

Yes ✓   No ✗

Restaurants (if service not included)	✓	10%
Cafés/bars (if service not included)	✓	10%
Hairdressers	✓	£1–£2
Taxis	✓	10%
Cloakroom attendants	✓	£1
Porters/Chambermaids	✓	£1 a bag/£2
Toilet attendants	✗	

POSTAL SERVICES

Each town and most large villages have at least one post office. Opening hours are 9–5.30 Mon–Fri and 9–12.30 Sat, closed Sun. Small offices close for lunch from 1–2pm. Stamps are also sold by some newspaper shops and shops selling postcards.

INTERNET

High-speed internet access is widely available in cities and larger towns although don't expect it in the more remote areas. While some hotels may offer free internet access it is more usual to be charged. Wireless broadband is increasingly available in hotels and city centre coffee shops.

TELEPHONES

Public telephones on the street and in bars, hotels and restaurants accept 10, 20, 50p, £1 and £2 coins, while others can only be used with phone cards (available from newspaper shops and post offices). Costs are considerably less expensive than using the phone in your hotel room.

International dialling codes

From the UK to:

France: 00 33	Spain: 00 34
Germany: 00 49	USA: 00 1
	Netherlands: 00 31

Emergency telephone number

Police, Fire, Ambulance: 999

CONSULATES AND HIGH COMMISSIONS (EDINBURGH)

USA ☎ 0131 556 8315	Netherlands ☎ 0131 220 3226
Germany ☎ 0131 337 2323	Spain ☎ 0131 220 1843

HEALTH ADVICE

Sun advice It is possible to get sunburn and sunstroke, particularly during the summer. Avoid prolonged exposure and use sunblock or cover up.

Drugs Prescription, non-prescription drugs and medicines are available from pharmacies. Non-prescription drugs and medicines are also widely available in supermarkets.

Safe water Tap water is generally safe to drink.

PERSONAL SAFETY

Theft from cars is unfortunately
common, as are the usual crimes
associated with big cities such as bag
snatching and pickpockets. Any crime
should be reported to the police and a
report requested if you plan to file an
insurance claim.

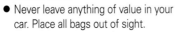

- Never leave anything of value in your
  car. Place all bags out of sight.
- Keep passports, tickets and valuables in a hotel safe deposit box.
- Avoid wearing a camera around your neck or displaying valuables.
- Wear your bag across your chest rather than over your shoulder.
- Don't walk alone in dimly lit areas at night.

ELECTRICITY

The electricity supply is 240 volts. Sockets take square three pin plugs.
All visitors from other countries will require an adaptor. American
appliances also require a voltage converter.

OPENING HOURS

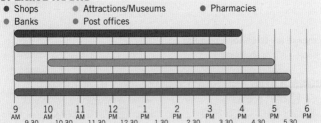

The above times are general and there are variations. Shops will usually
remain open throughout lunch and even on Sundays in the larger towns,
cities and tourist resorts. Supermarkets will also be open seven days and
close between 7pm and 10pm but several now offer 24-hour opening
Monday to Friday, mainly in the cities. Markets are generally open 8–4.
In rural areas shops will close for an hour at lunch time, generally 1–2pm,
for one afternoon each week and all day Sunday.

LANGUAGE

The language of the country is English but even English-speaking people may have some difficulties with the Scots language when specifically Scots words are used. These will vary according to region. In Aberdeen the dialect is known as Doric, in the Lowlands of Scotland it is Lallans, the city of Glasgow has a patter all of its own and in Orkney and Shetland the local dialect has Scandinavian roots. Although you may not wish to use the dialects, knowing the most common dialect words will ease understanding.

ashet a large serving dish

bannock a round flat cake cooked on a griddle

brose a type of porridge made from oats or pease-meal

bridie a spicy meat and onion pasty

butterie or **rowie** a croissant-like bread roll with lots of butter

caller fresh

clootie dumpling a rich fruit cake, boiled in a cloth

aye yes

naw no

ceilidh dance or party

greet to cry

bairn, chiel, wean child

hen, quine (NE), wifie, lassie girl or woman

jimmy, loon (NE), laddie man or boy

brae hill

burn a stream

glen valley

braw good

dreich overcast and dull

droukit soaked

glaur mud

dram a measure of whisky

drouth thirst

drouthy thirsty

gigot or **shank** a leg of lamb or pork; gigot is normally the thick end and shank the thin end

haggis dish made from offal, blood, oatmeal and spices, boiled in a sheep's stomach

tatties potatoes

champit tatties mashed potatoes

haiver to talk rubbish

ken to know

kenspeckle well known

muckle big

blether to gossip

crabbit bad-tempered

nyaff, scunner unpleasant person

greetin'-faced miserable person

kirk church

cairn a pile of stones used as a marker or memorial

gloaming evening

simmer dim mid-summer when it never gets quite dark but the sun just dips below the horizon

tattie scones flat scone made of potatoes and flour

tattie bogle scarecrow

stovies potatoes cooked with onion and a little meat

piece sandwich

play piece playtime snack

jeelie piece jam sandwich

piece break mid-morning break

girdle gridle or flat iron plate for cooking scones on top of the stove

messages shopping, normally for groceries

speir ask or enquire

stravaig to wander abroad

peelie wallie pale and wan

shilpit thin

sleekit sly

sonsie healthy looking

thrawn perverse

furth outside the area

sooth south; in Orkney and Shetland refers to the mainland

smirr just a little rain in the air

snell cold

stoating bouncing; used when describing heavy rain

Best places to see

1 Burns National Heritage Park

www.burnsheritagepark.com

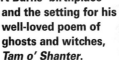

Alloway was Robert Burns' birthplace and the setting for his well-loved poem of ghosts and witches, *Tam o' Shanter*.

Robert Burns' father, William Burnes, built his 'auld clay biggin' near the banks of the River Doon, with walls 1m (3ft) thick and tiny windows to protect against the chill Scottish winters. This long, low, thatched cottage, where Robert was born, still stands today, restored to its original condition, at the heart of the Burns National Heritage Park. Among the fascinating memorabilia on display are a plaster cast of the poet's skull, his Bible, and various original manuscripts, including the world's most famous song of parting *Auld Lang Syne*.

The manuscript of *Tam o' Shanter*, also on view in the cottage, is translated into virtual reality at the nearby visitor centre in the Tam o' Shanter Experience. This hilarious and atmospheric tale recounts how the hapless Tam, in a drunken stupor, blunders upon the witches,

then entranced by the pretty young Nannie, roars out, 'Weel done Cutty sark!', only to be chased from Alloway Kirk to the Brig o' Doon by a 'hellish legion' of witches. The reality of 'Alloway's auld haunted kirk' is nearby and in this eerie ruin it is easy to imagine the open coffins and malignant tokens of the poem. Follow the chase from here to the Brig o' Doon, where Tam's mare Meg lost her tail to the winsome witch. This narrow old stone bridge was on the main road from Ayr to Carrick, a route well trodden by Burns, and gives some idea of the primitive state of Scotland's roads 200 years ago.

✚ 131 D5 ✉ Alloway
☎ 01292 443700
⏰ Apr–Oct daily 10–5.30
(10–5 in winter)
♿ Moderate 🍴 Tea room
(Jun–Sep, £) 🚌 Western 57
from Ayr to Alloway, hourly
🚆 Nearest train station Ayr

2 Burrell Collection

www.glasgowmuseums.com

This wonderful museum is built around an exquisite, idiosyncratic collection, gathered over a period of 80 years.

The millionaire shipping magnate Sir William Burrell left his eclectic collection of paintings, tapestries, stained glass, furniture, silver and precious objects to the people of Glasgow in 1944. He was a magpie who started collecting as a boy and continued until his death in 1958, by which time his acquisitions numbered some 8,000 treasures and objects from around the world.

For years the collection lay in storerooms until the present building in Pollok Country Park was constructed in 1983 to house it, enhancing it and adorned by it. This red sandstone, wood and glass structure nestles in a corner of the parkland next to a grove of chestnut and sycamore. Inside, the great glass walls bring the woodlands into the heart of the museum. Medieval stone doorways and windows have been built into the fabric of the building, antique stained glass hangs before the glass walls and the rooms are clad in ancient tapestries. Three rooms from Burrell's home at Hutton Castle have been re-created with their windows looking out on to the glass-roofed central courtyard. The collection is particularly strong on rare oriental porcelain and fine medieval French tapestries, but includes paintings by Cézanne and Degas and sculptures by Rodin. It is intriguing not just for the objects and the building but because of the man who assembled it.

✠ 139 A4 (off Map) ✉ Pollok Country Park, Glasgow
☎ 0141 287 2550 ◷ Mon–Thu, Sat, 10–5, Fri, Sun 11–5
✋ Free 🍴 Café (£) 🚌 45, 47, 48, 57 from central Glasgow
🚇 Pollokshaws West, then ten minutes' walk

3 Culloden Battlefield

www.nts.org.uk

This desolate moor, where the last battle on British soil was fought, was the scene of savage slaughter after the defeat of the Jacobites.

This bleak moorland has been restored to the condition it was in on that fateful morning in 1746 when the hopes of the Royal House of Stuart to regain the throne of Scotland were forever dashed. It is a melancholy site where, tradition has it, the birds never sing and where no heather grows on the graves of the clansmen slaughtered in the aftermath by the forces of the Duke of Cumberland.

The broad, windswept expanse of Culloden Moor was ideal for the government's cavalry and artillery – the entrenched guns laid waste the Highland ranks. When finally the Highlanders charged, they became bogged down in the mud and scattered in disorder. Their infantry, already outnumbered, exhausted and starving after the long march from Derby, faltered and fell under a murderous hail of shot. The wounded survivors were slaughtered where they lay, and indiscriminate butchery of men, women and children was encouraged by Cumberland on the road to Inverness. The following year, all weapons, bagpipes, tartan and the kilt were banned by law in a bid to destroy the Highland culture and the clan system. Today, the episode is described in an excellent audiovisual display in the visitor centre.

The Battle of Culloden was the last battle of the Jacobite rebellion of 1745, and the final defeat was followed by cruelty and years of persecution. An oppressive sadness and poignancy surrounds the memorial cairns, the sort of atmosphere that clings to such places as the Somme and Auschwitz that have witnessed pitiless waste of human life.

✚ 135 D6 ✉ 10km (6 miles) east of Inverness ☎ 01463 790607 🕐 Moor always open. Visitor centre daily Feb–end Mar 10–4; Apr–end Oct daily 9–6; Nov–end Dec daily 10–4. Closed Christmas and Jan ✋ Moderate 🍴 Restaurant 'Tastes of Scotland' (£–££) 🚌 Highland Country Buses from Inverness (the No. 7 bus)

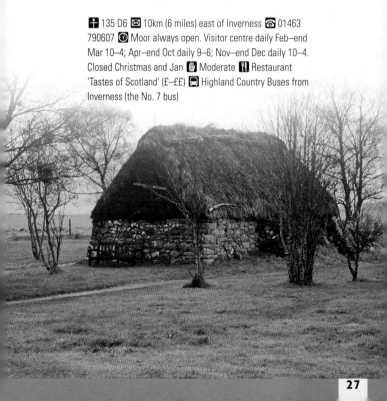

4 Edinburgh Castle

www.historic-scotland.gov.uk

Home to monarchs, scene of banquets and siege, this castle is not only at the heart of Scotland's capital but of its history.

Edinburgh Castle dominates the city from every angle and is visible from miles away. Over a million people visit every year and the queues for the Crown Room start to form early every day. The ancient Honours of Scotland are the oldest crown jewels in Europe, and the Stone of Destiny on which all Scots monarchs were crowned is also on display here.

There's been a fortification on this great volcanic rock since Celtic times, and the tiny Norman St. Margaret's Chapel, the oldest building in Edinburgh, has stood intact for more than 900 years. The newly restored Royal Apartments include the room where Mary, Queen of Scots gave birth to the future James VI of Scotland (James I of England). The Great Hall has seen many historic gatherings and is still used for receptions by the Scottish First Minister. In the castle's cellar is the colossal cannon called Mons Meg, which fired its massive stone cannonballs at the Battle of Flodden in 1513, a devastating defeat for the Scots by the English. At 1pm you can witness the firing of the one o'clock gun – not Mons Meg! The

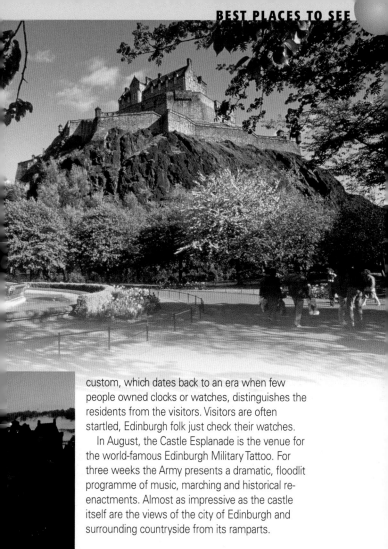

custom, which dates back to an era when few people owned clocks or watches, distinguishes the residents from the visitors. Visitors are often startled, Edinburgh folk just check their watches.

In August, the Castle Esplanade is the venue for the world-famous Edinburgh Military Tattoo. For three weeks the Army presents a dramatic, floodlit programme of music, marching and historical re-enactments. Almost as impressive as the castle itself are the views of the city of Edinburgh and surrounding countryside from its ramparts.

✚ 140 A3 ✉ Top of the Royal Mile ☎ 0131 225 9846
⏱ Apr–end Oct daily 9.30–6 (5 in winter) ✋ Expensive
🍴 Cafés (£–££) 🚊 Waverley

5 Glen Coe

This majestic mountain pass running from Glencoe village to Rannoch Moor is one of the most spectacular and dramatic sights in Scotland.

Lying at the foot of massive mountains, often disappearing into heavy swirling cloud, the gloom in Glen Coe can be oppressive. Under clear blue skies, the smooth green humps of the mountains, the rocky summits of the Three Sisters, the wide floor of the glen and the distant mountain tops beyond are a familiar sight the world over on calendars and in films. *Braveheart*, *Restless Natives*, *Highlander* and many other movies were shot in the Glen.

There is an awesome stillness about the Glen, which even the great numbers of tourists, walkers and climbers never disturb. However, its peace was rudely shattered on a winter morning more than 300 years ago when Glen Coe became a byword

for treachery. The chief of the Clan MacDonald was late in swearing allegiance to the Crown. Campbell of Glenlyon, under orders signed by King William, took his men to Glencoe to make an example of the MacDonalds. He billeted his men there on the pretext that they were just passing through. In the early dawn of 13 February 1692, throughout the glen, the Campbells dragged MacDonald men from their beds and murdered them, burning the houses as they went. The women, some carrying infants, fled into the mountains in a piercing snowstorm, many perishing miserably.

Nowadays the unpredictable weather still claims lives among the skiers, walkers and climbers who flock to the Glen. There are countless challenging walks and climbs, but this is no land for a casual afternoon stroll.

In summer a trip up the ski lift to the summit will be rewarded by spectacular views over Rannoch Moor and the surrounding mountains.

➕ 135 F5 ✉ 24km (15 miles) south of Fort William
🍴 Snack bar in Glencoe Village (£) 🚌 Scottish City Link from Glasgow and Fort William

6 New Lanark

www.newlanark.org

New Lanark was the first example of a working environment planned to consider the welfare of the workforce as well as efficiency and profit.

Designated a World Heritage Site in 2001, this was Robert Owen's utopian village, built near the Falls of Clyde to harness the power of the water for driving the cotton mills. New Lanark was much more than a mill town; it was a model village, and Owen (1771–1858) was the forerunner of the great Victorian philanthropists who built towns such as Saltaire and Port Sunlight. Contrary to the wisdom of the time, Owen believed that a happy workforce would be a productive workforce, so he provided modern housing, a shop, a school and recreation facilities. His employees also worked shorter hours and had better working conditions, schooling was compulsory and he did not employ children under 10 in the mill.

His competitors thought he was crazy and that his business would suffer. They were astonished when it became even more profitable. New Lanark survived as a mill town

into the 20th century and was saved from ultimate demolition when it was restored as a conservation project. You can tour the houses, gardens and recreation hall, see the restored looms working and learn about life at the time through the eyes of a young girl in the Annie McLeod Experience.

Although it is in the industrial heartland of Scotland, New Lanark is set in a rural location by the Clyde. This was part of Owen's plan that his workers should live in pleasant surroundings. You can follow the delightful riverside walk to the Falls of Clyde to appreciate the importance of this.

✚ 131 C6 ✉ In a gorge below Lanark ☎ 01555 661345
🕐 Jun–end Aug daily 10.30–5; Sep–Jun daily 11–5
✋ Moderate 🍽 Tea room (£) 🚌 Bus service from station in Lanark 🚃 Lanark
ℹ Horsemarket, Ladyacre Road, Lanark ☎ 01555 661661

7 Rosslyn Chapel

www.rosslynchapel.org.uk

This tiny, atmospheric medieval chapel is an exquisite masterpiece of the mason's art, with an unrivalled range and delicacy of carving.

Rosslyn Chapel is possibly the most mysterious building in Scotland, like a great medieval cathedral in miniature. It is richly carved, including the most complete *danse macabre* (dance of death) in Europe and the death mask of King Robert the Bruce, reproduced in stone. Built by Sir William St. Clair, it has strong connections with the Knights Templar, a mystical order of wealthy warrior monks, who fought with Robert the Bruce at Bannockburn (1314). They were credited with finding the Holy Grail and the treasures of Solomon.

It is said that the Holy Grail is hidden in the great Apprentice Pillar. The story goes that the apprentice saw the pillar in a dream and carved it in his master's absence. The master was so jealous

when he saw the work that he felled the apprentice with a single blow of his mallet. The master was hanged, and his effigy and that of the apprentice and his mother can be found close to the pillars. Whatever the truth, there is no doubt that the master masons who chiselled these intricate patterns and medieval likenesses were exceptionally gifted.

Whether it is the medieval faces peering out of the stone on all sides or the 20 knights in full armour interred below, there is a supernatural feel to this tiny chapel and a strange chill as you enter the crypt. The chapel has found recent fame through its connection with the best-selling novel *The Da Vinci Code* by Dan Brown.

✚ 131 C7 ✉ Off Chapel Loan, opposite The Roslin Glen Hotel, Roslin (11km/7 miles south of Edinburgh) ☎ 0131 440 2159 🕐 Apr–end Sep Mon–Sat 9.30–6; Oct–end Mar Mon–Sat 9.30–5; Sun 12–4.45 all year 💷 Moderate 🍴 Coffee shop (£) 🚌 62 (First); 15A and 62 (Lothian) from Edinburgh

8 Skara Brae

www.historic-scotland.gov.uk

On a beautiful sandy seashore on the edge of the world is the perfectly preserved neolithic settlement of Skara Brae in Orkney.

Buried for centuries under the sand dunes of the Bay of Skail, a great storm in 1850 uncovered this Stone Age village, which has been excavated.

The villagers dug holes into the sandy soil so that their homes were half underground, affording some

protection against the winds. Interconnecting passages between the huts were lined with sandstone slabs. Wandering around the site and looking down into these homes is a poignant experience. The layout of the rooms resembles any small peasant dwelling – except everything here, including the furniture, is made of stone. The dresser is a couple of flagstone shelves resting on stone 'legs', the bed is made of three slabs of stone set against the wall to form a 'box', and there is a central hearth.

There are few trees on Orkney, which is why the people of Skara Brae had to use alternative materials. Whale jawbones were probably used as rafters to support the roof, tools were made of bone and stone, and pottery was richly decorated. These ancient people were farmers who bred cows and sheep and grew grains. Looking into their homes makes their lives seem vivid and close. An excellent reconstruction of a stone house complete with a roof is well worth a visit.

✚ 138 E1 ✉ 13km (8 miles) north of Stromness, Orkney ⏰ Apr–end Sep Mon–Sun 9.30–5.30; Oct–end Mar Mon–Sun 9–4.30 👣 Moderate 🍽 Café (£) ℹ️ Visitor centre ☎ 01856 841815

9 The Tenement House, Glasgow

www.nts.org.uk

Most of the population of industrial Scotland in the 19th and early 20th centuries lived in four- or five-storey tenement buildings similar to this one.

Miss Agnes Toward moved into this three-roomed flat with her mother in 1911 and lived there until her death in 1965. Houses in tenements ranged from the single end, which would nowadays be called a studio flat, to apartments such as this one, with several bedrooms and even a bathroom. Most apartments had no inside toilet but several families would share one toilet off the stairs. Better classes of tenement building were distinguished by the 'wally close', with ornate patterned ceramic tiles on the walls of the entry.

The kitchen of a tenement, with the cooking range for warmth, was the hub of family life. Miss Toward's kitchen utensils lie on the deal (fir or pine) table, her jars of home-made jam are still sealed above, the washboard is in the deep ceramic sink and the washing hangs to dry on the pulley. The bed, built into the recess in the kitchen, consists of a lumpy mattress on boards and snow-white bed linen, and there is a another bed tucked away below to accommodate the large families which were the norm.

When Miss Toward died it was discovered that she had never thrown anything away. She had kept bus tickets, letters booking her holidays, even newspapers, which were piled high on chairs and tables. It was a significant hoard of ephemera, portraying a way of life that was passing, a tiny fragment of history caught in amber, and nostalgia for those who can remember it.

✚ 139 C2 ✉ 145 Buccleuch Street, Glasgow
☎ 0141 333 0183 ⏱ Mar–end Oct daily 1–5 (last entry 4.30) ✋ Moderate 🚌 From Buchanan Street Bus Station
🚇 Charing Cross

39

10 Traquair House

www.traquair.co.uk

Dating from the early 12th century, Traquair claims to be the oldest continually inhabited house in Scotland.

The house was originally built as a hunting lodge for the Scottish kings and queens. Because of its strategic position on the banks of the River Tweed, it was fortified against border raids. James III gave it to his court musician, who sold it to the Earl of Buchan for £3 15s. Buchan's son James Stuart became the first laird, and from then on it developed as a family home. The main section was completed around 1600 and another two wings were added a century later. The famous Bear Gates were erected in 1737 at a cost of £12 15s for the pillars, £10 4s for the carving of the stone bears and four gallons of ale for the workmen. The gates opened into a long tree-lined avenue which Prince Charles Edward Stuart trod one late autumn day in

1745 as he set off on his ill-fated venture to try to reclaim the throne for the House of Stuart. The Earl swore that they would never be opened again until a Stuart returned to the throne of Scotland. To this day they remain sealed.

The woodlands and gardens around Traquair are usually buzzing with activity – there are various craft

workshops and a brewery. The beer is brewed in the old brew-house and fermented in 200-year-old oak casks. The maze next to the house is a delight for children, while the house itself is a labyrinth, with lots of quirky little steps and corridors and secret passages. Above all, it still has the feel of a family home.

➕ 131 C7 ✉ 2km (1.5 miles) south of Innerleithen ☎ 01896 830323 🕐 Jun–end Aug daily 10.30–5; Apr, May, Sep daily 12–5; Oct daily 11–4; Nov weekends 11–3 (guided tours). Last admissions half an hour before closing 🏷 Moderate 🍴 Tea room (£) 🚌 62 from Edinburgh and Peebles to Innerleithen

Exploring

Scotland occupies the upper third of Britain and some Scots would argue that the best has risen to the top. Certainly, it is geographically blessed: Britain's highest mountains, largest national park and deepest lakes are in Scotland. But it is also historically and culturally rich. Few nationalities have as distinctive an identity as the Scots and their world-famous exports whisky, golf and tartan – although haggis seems not to have caught on. Politically and historically, Edinburgh, the home of the Scottish Parliament, dominates Scottish life. But its rival to the west, Glasgow, has as much to offer culture vultures, with its unique architectural heritage. To appreciate the best of Scotland you should get off the beaten track: seek out remote seaside towns on the west coast where some of the most beautiful beaches in Europe lie, venture into the heather-clad Highlands or take a ferry to Scotland's enchanting islands.

Edinburgh and the Borders

Built on a series of volcanic rocks, Scotland's capital is undoubtedly one of the most beautiful cities of Europe. Few sights can compare with Princes Street Gardens laid out beneath the castle, massive on its dark crag.

Edinburgh

During the many wars with England, Edinburgh Castle was often the destination of the English armies and the area between the castle and the border was laid waste time and again. Even in times of peace, cross-border raids by cattle reivers (thieves) meant that the inhabitants of this region could never relax, but it was also an

area of prosperity. Huge castles, built for defence, became grand dwellings of the aristocracy in times of peace. As you drive, bicycle or walk through the rolling hills of the borders or along the rivers Yarrow, Tweed and Ettrick, the tranquillity belies its violent past.

EDINBURGH

Edinburgh is a city of two towns. Beside the castle are the narrow closes, winding streets and tall tenements of the Old Town, while opposite are the elegant classical squares, broad streets and peaceful gardens of the Georgian New Town. It's a joy to walk round this rich architectural tapestry, to stroll through gardens where suddenly the city bustle disappears into greenery and birdsong, or to climb the many hills and capture a glimpse of the Firth of Forth or majestic Arthur's Seat, and another perspective of this incomparable city.

Britannia

Since the former royal yacht opened to the public at the Port of Leith in 1998, it has become Edinburgh's second-biggest attraction after the castle. There is an excellent visitor centre with exhibits of photos and reconstructed crews' cabins, but the real enticement is the yacht itself. You can see the Queen's bedroom, the royal sitting rooms and magnificent state rooms that have witnessed many international receptions.
www.royalyachtbritannia.co.uk

✚ 140 D1 (off map) ✉ Ocean Drive, Leith ☎ 0131 555 5566 🕓 Apr–end Sep daily 9.30–4.30; Oct–end Mar daily 10–3.30 👋 Expensive 🍴 Excellent café (£) ❓ Reserve in advance

Calton Hill

Calton Hill is a superb vantage point from which to view the city, the Firth of Forth and the kingdom of Fife beyond. On Friday evenings you can also see the stars as the City Observatory is open to the public. The remainder of the buildings on Calton Hill are very curious structures: the Nelson Monument is a telescope-

shaped tower, while the uncompleted Greek temple is the National Monument to all those that were killed in the Napoleonic Wars.

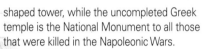 140 D1 ❓ The City Observatory is open some Friday evenings 8–10, subject to the keyholder and a clear sky ☎ 0131 556 4365 after 5pm on Friday

Edinburgh Castle
Best places to see, ➤ 28–29.

Grassmarket
Edinburgh's first market area built outside the city walls has seen many changes. From marketplace to public execution site, it became a depressed slum area, frequented by down-and-outs. However, its fortunes have revived and it is now a cosmopolitan area with an eclectic mix of shops and pubs. Stan Wood, Britain's only commercial palaeontologist, has his fossil shop at 5 Cowgatehead. Among the bright façades in Victoria Street are a brush shop, a traditional cheesemonger, a French baker and a great indoor flea market called Byzantium.

✚ 140 B3 🍴 Excellent cafés (£) and restaurants (££–£££) on the square

Museum of Scotland

Edinburgh's latest addition merges a bold modern design with the vaulted hall, cast-iron balconies and glass roof of the Royal Museum of Scotland to which it is adjoined. Displays are built into the walls, and by the tantalizing use of arches and gaps, discrete spaces are created. Unlike the Royal Museum, which in true Victorian style has a wonderful miscellaneous selection of exhibits and curiosities from across the globe, the new museum focuses on Scotland. The whole of Scotland's story, from prehistoric rocks and fossils to the late 20th century, unfolds here. One of the more gruesome displays is the early Scottish guillotine, the Iron Maiden, along with the names of some of those who lost their heads to it. Among the exhibits in the display of 20th-century items representative of the century is a Fender Stratocaster guitar, chosen by the former Prime Minister, Tony Blair.

www.nms.ac.uk

✚ 140 C4 ✉ Chambers Street
☎ 0131 247 4422 🕐 Daily 10–5
✋ Free 🍴 Excellent café (£) and high-class restaurant (£££) on premises

Palace of Holyroodhouse

At the bottom of the spine of volcanic rock known as the Royal Mile is Holyroodhouse Palace, home of Scottish monarchs since the 16th century, although most of the current building dates from 1671. It was here that Mary, Queen of Scots, spent much of her short reign, and where she suffered the tirades of John Knox and witnessed the savage slaughter of her servant Riccio.

The Palace of Holyrood is the Queen's official residence in Scotland, but the state and historic apartments are open to the public.

Spreading out behind the palace, **Holyrood Park** is dominated by the great volcanic plug known as Arthur's Seat. A climb to the top is rewarded with stunning views of Edinburgh, Fife and the Borders, and there are paths for walking or bicycling. Rock climbers and abseilers practise on Salisbury Crags, and you can picnic by the pond. Cars are prohibited on Sunday.
www.royal.gov.uk

✚ 140 F2 ✉ Canongate, Royal Mile ☎ 0131 556 5100 🕓 Palace Apr–end Oct daily 9.30–6; Nov–end Mar 9.30–4:30 (closed when the Queen is in residence; telephone to check). Last admission one hour before closing. Gardens open during summer ♿ Expensive 🍴 Excellent tea room (£) up Royal Mile

Holyrood Park
🕓 Open all hours 🍴 Excellent cafés/restaurants on the Royal Mile (£)

The People's Story

Situated in the former Canongate Tolbooth on the Royal Mile, this fascinating free museum of social history is one of the gems of Edinburgh. Re-creations of living quarters, workshops and displays of objects seek to explain the manner and quality of life for ordinary Edinburgh folk over the years.
www.cac.org.uk

✚ 140 E2 ✉ Canongate Tolbooth, 163 Canongate
☎ 0131 529 4057 ⊗ Mon–Sat 10–5 (Sun 12–5 during Aug only) 🖐 Free 🍴 Excellent café (£) across street

Princes Street

One of the great joys of shopping in Princes Street is the space. Only one side of the street has buildings, the other side is Princes Street Gardens (➤ below), where you can escape the crowds. Jenner's, with its labyrinth of departments and tiers of polished balconies, is the world's oldest independent department store. If you tire of shopping, slip out the back door onto Rose Street, which has more pubs than any other street in Scotland.

✚ 140 A2 🍴 Excellent cafés/bars in Rose Street (£–£££)

Princes Street Gardens

It is hard to believe that these carefully tended gardens were once the Nor' Loch (north loch), into which ran all the sewage of the Old Town. The gardens run the length of Princes Street, divided into two parts by the Mound, the pile of earth excavated when the New Town was built. The Greek grandeur of the Royal Scottish Academy and the National Gallery of Scotland now occupy the site. There's a bandstand for summer concerts and an open-air café. On the last night of the Festival, the spectacular Bank of Scotland Fireworks Concert is staged here, and at New Year it hosts the world's biggest Hogmanay (New Year's Eve) party.

✚ 140 A2 🍴 Snack bar in gardens (£)

Scottish National Portrait Gallery

In a Gothic red sandstone building, this gallery offers a fascinating tour of the great and the good of Scotland past and present. Among the kings and queens in the collection are portraits of Mary, Queen of Scots, as well as her persecutor John Knox and her ill-fated husband Lord Darnley. Robert Burns, J. M. Barrie and Hugh McDiarmid are among the literary greats.

www.nationalgalleries.org

✚ 140 C1 ✉ Junction of Queen Street and St. Andrews Street

☎ 0131 624 6200 🕓 Mon–Sun 10–5 (Thu 10–7) ♿ Free 🍴 Café (£)

The Scottish Parliament

After a break of nearly 300 years, Scotland again has its own Parliament. From 1999 it was in temporary accommodation in the Church of Scotland Assembly. In October 2004 it moved to its new home, a futuristic building adjacent to the Palace of

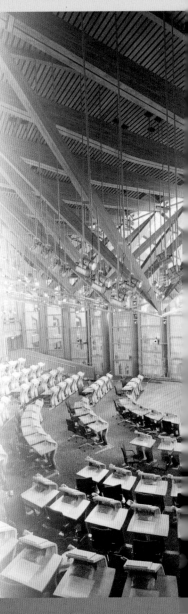

Holyroodhouse. It was designed by Spanish architect Enric Miralles, in a fusion of Catalan and Scottish styles.

www.scottish-parliament.uk

➕ 140 F2 ✉ Holyrood Road ☎ 0131 348 5200 🕐 Tue–Thu 9–7 (business days); Apr–Oct Mon, Fri 10–6; Nov–Mar Mon, Fri 10–4; Sat, Sun 10–4 all year ♿ Free; guided tours moderate 🍴 Café (£)

The Borders

ABBOTSFORD HOUSE

Sir Walter Scott (1771–1832) designed Abbotsford and lived there until his death. The Scots Baronial design, with medieval towers and turrets, reflects his romantic side. The library, housing Scott's rare books, is light and airy and also displays his accumulation of bizarre Scottish memorabilia, from Bonnie Prince Charlie's hair to the crucifix carried by Mary, Queen of Scots, when she was beheaded.

www.scottsabbotsford.co.uk

➕ 131 C8 ✉ 3km (2 miles) west of Melrose ☎ 01896 752043 🕐 Mid-Mar to end Oct daily 9.30–5 (Mar–end May and Oct, Sun 2–5); Nov to mid-Mar Mon–Fri group by appointment only ♿ Moderate 🍴 Tea room (£)

HADDINGTON

The historic town of Haddington, a mixture of broad tree-lined streets and medieval street plan, is an architectural delight. The High Street, with its lanes, narrow alleys and quaint shops, is fronted by the elegant Town House designed by William Adam. Nearby is the classical frontage of Carlyle House. The childhood home of Jane Welsh Carlyle, wife of Thomas Carlyle, the Sage of Chelsea, is tucked away behind it. Around the corner lies Haddington House, the oldest house in town, complete with re-created 17th-century garden. Further on, the tranquil riverside walk leads to St. Mary's Collegiate Church, steeped in historical significance. The marks of the bombardment by the English during the 'Rough Wooing' are still visible. John Knox, the great Protestant reformer, preached here; the Lauderdale Aisle is an exquisite Episcopalian chapel; and two of the lovely stained-glass windows are by Sir Edward Burne-Jones.

Just beyond Haddington is **Lennoxlove,** set in 240ha (593 acres) of verdant woodlands. It appears to have grown in a mixture of styles around a medieval tower and has a collection of furniture, paintings and mementoes of Mary, Queen of Scots, including her death mask. A year-long renovation ended in 2007.

✚ 131 B8

Lennoxlove

✉ 3km (2 miles) south of Haddington ☎ 01620 823720; www.lennoxlove.org
🕓 Apr–end Oct Wed, Thu and Sun 11.30–3 half hourly tours 🖐 Moderate

JEDBURGH

This lovely little town with its old wynds (alleys) and houses was established as a Royal Burgh in the 12th century. The immense, graceful ruin of Jedburgh Abbey, founded in 1138, gives the most complete impression of all the Border abbeys' great monastic

institutions. It has a haunting abandoned feel to it, as if its medieval inhabitants might return next week to repair the roof. The

mellow 16th-century tower house, known as Mary Queen of Scots' House, is worth a visit, too. It wasn't actually her house but she did stay here.

www.historic-scotland.gov.uk

✚ 131 D8 ✉ 16km (10 miles) southwest of Kelso ☎ 01835 863925
🕓 Apr–end Sep daily 9.30–5.30; Oct–end Mar Mon–Sat 9.30–4.30
🖐 Inexpensive 🍴 Cafés and restaurants (£) nearby ❓ Times apply to Dryburgh and Melrose abbeys, too

KELSO

The small market town of Kelso has an enormous cobbled square with a cluster of Georgian houses around it and a maze of cobbled streets leading off. Kelso Abbey suffered badly during the 'Rough Wooing' when Henry VIII tried to control the infant Mary, Queen of Scots, and not much remains. Floors Castle, a mile along the Cobby Riverside walk, is an early 18th-century mansion designed by William Adam and still home to the Duke of Roxburgh.

Mellerstain House, a few miles away, is possibly the finest Georgian mansion in Scotland, retaining the original tones in its interior paintwork. Allow half a day to take in the superb collection of paintings, period furniture and terraced gardens.

➕ 131 C8

Mellerstain House

✉ Gordon ☎ 01573 410225; www.mellerstain.com ⏰ May, Jun, Sep Wed; Jul, Aug Sun, Mon, Wed, Thu 12.30–5; Oct Sun only 12.30–5. Closed Nov–end Apr 💷 Moderate 🍴 Restaurant (££)

MELROSE

Nestling in the Eildon Hills, Melrose is yet another picturesque old abbey town. The heart of Robert the Bruce, who rebuilt the abbey, is buried here. Nearby is a Roman three-hill fort, at Newstead, and the **Trimontium Exhibition** in Market Square tells that story.

🕂 131 C8

Trimontium Exhibition

✉ The Ormiston, Market Square ☎ 01896 822651; www.trimontium.net

🕐 Apr–end Oct daily 10.30–4.30 👜 Inexpensive 🍴 Restaurants (£) nearby

ROBERT SMAIL'S PRINTING WORKS, INNERLEITHEN

Robert Smail's High Street printing shop is perfectly preserved. There are lots of working exhibits, some of them hands-on.

www.nts.org.uk

🕂 131 C8 ✉ 7–9 High Street, Innerleithen ☎ 01896 830206 🕐 Apr–end Oct, Mon, Thu–Sat 12–5, Sun 1–5 👜 Moderate 🍴 Cafés and restaurants (£) nearby

a drive in Edinburgh and the Borders

From Princes Street head east along Waterloo Place and Regent Road, then turn right into London Road (A1). Follow it until you see signs for Haddington (▶ 54–55). Turn right and when your visit is completed, return to the A1 and follow the signs for Berwick-upon-Tweed. After 32km (20 miles), turn left on to the A1107 for Eyemouth, then at Coldingham take a left on to the B6438 to St. Abbs. Return via the B6438 to the A1, then turn left and continue until the turning for Duns on the A6105.

Chirnside, which you will pass, was the home of local farmer Jim Clark (1936–68) who was the world motor racing champion twice in the 1960s. Duns, the next town, has a museum dedicated to his life (44 Newtown Street).

From Duns follow the A6105 to its intersection with the A68, turn left and then in a short distance turn right on to the A6091 until you reach Galashiels, where you need to turn left on to the A72.

At Innerleithen you will find Robert Smail's Printing Works (► 57), and nearby is Traquair House (► 40–41).

Continue on the A72 until it joins the A702 just beyond Skirling. Turn left for Biggar.

In Biggar is the last gas works in Scotland, preserved as a museum; Gladstone Court, an indoor museum of old shops; and the Biggar Puppet Theatre.

Leave Biggar (A702) heading back the way you came, toward Edinburgh. After 29km (18 miles), turn right on to the A766 for Penicuick.

Here you will find the Edinburgh Crystal Visitor Centre.

Take the A701 from Penicuik, follow the signs for Roslin village and Rosslyn Chapel (► 34–38), then return to the A701 and follow the signs back to Edinburgh.

Distance 265km (165 miles)
Time 6–8 hours, depending on stops
Start point Princes Street ✚ 140 A2
Endpoint Edinburgh ✚ 131 B7
Lunch Tontine Hotel (££) ✉ High Street, Peebles (after Innerleithen)

ROSSLYN CHAPEL

Best places to see, ➤ 34–35.

ST. ABBS

St Abbs is a working fishing village. You can take a boat trip to get a closer look at the guillemots, kittiwakes, fulmars and razorbills that sweep and squeal and nest around the surrounding rocks and cliffs. Diving, to view the spectacular underwater scenery and sea life in these clear waters, is also possible. The nature reserve, near the village, offers rock-pool rambles and armchair dives, or you can follow the footpath to the lighthouse to appreciate the wonderful coastline and bird life.

✚ 133 B5 🍴 Café (£) near waterfront

TRAQUAIR HOUSE

Best places to see, ➤ 40–41.

Glasgow and the Southwest

Glasgow is a fine Victorian city, built on the fortunes of the British Empire. Edinburgh may be the capital of Scotland but Glasgow is its soul. The inhabitants are compulsively outgoing and gregarious so this is not a city to visit if you want to be alone. Sit on a park bench in George Square and within minutes someone will engage you in conversation.

In this area you will find the industrial heart of Scotland, the shipyards of the Clyde, fast-moving computer production, sleepy rural backwaters, the wildernesses of Galloway and miles of coastline. It is a microcosm of Scottish industry, history and literature. Two popular poets, penicillin, tarmacadam, the mackintosh, the bicycle and the pneumatic tyre, not to mention Robert the Bruce and William Wallace, all emerged from the southwest of Scotland.

GLASGOW

Since its portrayal in Alexander McArthur and Kingsley Long's 1935 novel *No Mean City* as a wild, gangster-dominated place, Glasgow has reinvented itself several times. The Garden Festival transformed the derelict dock areas along the Clyde, while The European City of Culture and City of Architecture 1999 proclaimed the stylishness of Glasgow.

World-renowned architects such as Charles Rennie Mackintosh and Alexander 'Greek' Thomson produced what has become one of Europe's best preserved Victorian cities. Imaginative modern designs, including the Burrell Collection and the Armadillo (the Scottish Exhibition and Conference Centre, a modern venue on the banks of the Clyde), maintain the standard while 1960s and 1970s architectural blight gradually disappears.

Burrell Collection
Best places to see, ➤ 24–25.

Gallery of Modern Art
This popular and witty gallery has undermined even the worthy statue of Wellington that fronts it. The great man and his horse are constantly adorned with traffic cones for headgear. In the entrance, the irreverent tone is set by the brilliant, papier mâché caricature of the Queen as a Glasgow housewife, in dressing gown and slippers, with dangling cigarette. The collection of art by living artists is housed on four floors.

www.glasgowmuseums.com

✚ 139 D2 ✉ Queen Street ☎ 0141 229 1996 ◷ Mon–Wed, Sat 10–5, Thu 10–8, Fri, Sun from 11–5 ✋ Free ⊮ Excellent café (£) on premises

Glasgow School of Art

Charles Rennie Mackintosh won the competition to design the new school in 1896. It is the earliest example in the UK of a complete art nouveau building, including the interior furnishings and fittings. Students today still remove books from Mackintosh bookcases and sit on priceless Mackintosh chairs.

www.gsa.ac.uk

🕇 139 C2 ✉ 167 Renfrew Street
☎ 0141 353 4526 ⊕ Guided tours only Mon–Fri 11, 2, Sat 10.30, 11.30; extra tours Apr–end Sep daily 11, 1.30, 2, 2.30 🖑 Moderate 🍴 Mackintosh's Willow Tea Room (£) is nearby at 217 Sauchiehall Street

Holmwood House

Restored by the National Trust for Scotland, Holmwood House, designed by Alexander 'Greek' Thomson, is one of Scotland's finest private villas. The paper magnate James Couper gave Thomson a free hand and he devised an astonishing asymmetrical design. One side has a flat classical frontage with pillars framing the dining room windows while the bay window on the other side is essentially a circular Greek temple, complete with free-standing pillars, fronting a timber and glass wall. None of the furniture remains but underneath the layers of paper, a remarkable amount of the original paint work has survived, including painted scenes of the Trojan Wars.

www.nts.org.uk

✚ 139 D4 ✉ 61 Netherlee Road, Cathcart ☎ 0141 637 2129
🕐 Apr–end Oct Thu–Mon 12–5 ✋ Moderate 🍴 Refreshments in Kitchen Court (£) 🚌 44 🚃 Glasgow Central (Neilston train to Cathcart station)

Kelvingrove Art Gallery and Museum

This elaborately turreted mansion, built of red Dumfriesshire sandstone stands on the banks of the River Kelvin. Its art collection includes works by Botticelli, the Pre-Raphaelites, the Impressionists and David Hockney, as well as many great Scottish artists, such as the Glasgow Boys (➤ 73). The museum has collections ranging from Egyptology and prehistory to ship-building and natural history and a Mini Museum for under 5s.

www.glasgowmuseums.com

✛ 139 B1 ✉ Argyll Street ☎ 0141 287 2699 🕐 Mon–Thu, Sat 10–5, Fri, Sun 11–5 🚇 Kelvinhall

Museum of Transport

Displays cover the history of Scottish transportation, including the pioneer days of the Scottish motor industry. Cars include early Arrol Johnstones produced in Dumfries and the Hillman Imp, built at the long-closed Chrysler plant at Linwood. There is also a series of trams, the famous 'Shooglies', the earliest with gleaming brass and polished wood, as well as a 1938 street scene with a working cinema and a Victorian underground station.

www.glasgowmuseums.com

✛ 139 B1 ✉ 1 Bunhouse Road ☎ 0141 287 2720 🕐 Mon, Thu, Sat 10–5, Fri, Sun 11–5 ✋ Free 🍴 Café (£)

Scotland Street School Museum

Designed by Charles Rennie Mackintosh, this is an architectural gem, featuring two massive glass-fronted towers. Inside it recreates the school experience of Scots children from Victorian times through to the 1950s. Classrooms have been reconstructed for several of the periods and, during school terms, visitors in the viewing galleries can watch local children and their teachers dress up in period costume and experience what it was like. Modern kids sometimes feel strange as their friendly teacher is transformed into the dragon of the Victorian classroom. At play time the youngsters take part in games from yesteryear. There are wooden spinning tops and girds and cleeks (hoops and sticks). The only problem for children is keeping the toys from the grown-ups.

www.glasgowmuseums.com

139 C4 225 Scotland Street 0141 287 0500 Apr–end Aug Mon–Thu and Sat 10–5, Fri and Sun 11–5 Free Café and vending machine area (£)

The Tall Ship at Glasgow Harbour

The River Clyde dominated world ship-building well into the 20th century. Many of the legendary liners, the *Queen Mary*, *Queen Elizabeth* and the *QE2*, were built here as well as other less famous ships. *The Glenlee* (1896) is one of the last of the Clyde-built sailing ships and one of only six still afloat. It was in the service of the Spanish navy until the 1970s. Acquired by the Clyde Maritime Trust, which has spent years restoring it, this steel-hulled cargo ship is one of Glasgow's newest attractions.

www.thetallship.com

139 B2 Yorkhill Quay, 100 Stobcross Road 0141 222 2513 Mar–end Oct daily 10–5; Nov–end Feb daily 10–4 Moderate Café (£)

The Tenement House, Glasgow

Best places to see, ➤ 38–39.

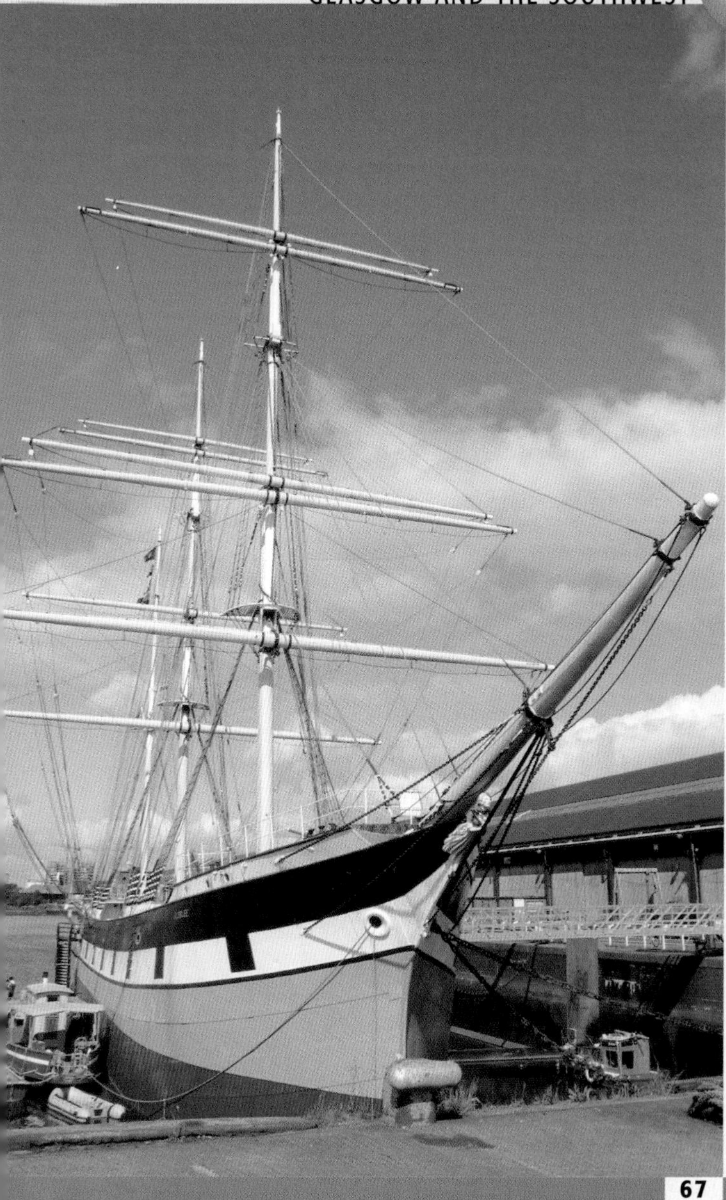

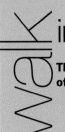

a walk in central Glasgow

This walk around central Glasgow takes in some of the city's most interesting architecture.

From the tourist office in George Square turn right then right onto Miller Street, left along Ingram Street and right on to Glassford Street.

The Tobacco Lairds House is on Miller Street. Glasgow's oldest secular building is the Trades Hall in Glassford Street, designed by Robert Adam in 1794.

Turn left onto Wilson Street, right at Candleriggs and left along the Trongate. Turn right on to Saltmarket and left on to Glasgow Green. Follow paths to the People's Palace and beyond that to Templeton Business Centre.

Modelled on the Palazzo Ducale in Venice, the multi-hued, richly patterned Templeton Business Centre was originally a Victorian carpet factory.

Return to the gates of Glasgow Green and go along Clyde Street. Turn right on to Jamaica Street, right on to Howard Street and left to St Enoch Square. Across Argyle Street head along Buchanan Street. Walk around Royal Exchange Square on the right. Continue on Buchanan Street then left along St. Vincent Street.

In St. Enoch Square the former underground station resembles a miniature château. St. Vincent Street Church is the only surviving church of the Victorian architect Alexander 'Greek' Thomson.

Turn right up Pitt Street and right on to Renfrew Street, right at Dalhousie Street and left on Sauchiehall Street.

In Sauchiehall Street is another Thomson design, the former Grecian Chambers, and the Willow Tea Rooms, owned by Kate Cranston.

At Buchanan Street turn right, then left along West George Street to return to George Square.

Distance 5–6km (3–4 miles)
Time 4 hours
Start/end point George Square ➕ 139 D2
Lunch 78 St. Vincent Street

The Southwest

ARRAN

Reached by Calmac ferry from Gourock, Arran is a delight. The
main town of Brodick with its castle and gardens can be explored
in a day trip, but it will take a few days to visit the standing stones
on Machrie Moor, climb Goatfell or watch the sunset over Ailsa
Craig from the south coast. Pottery, paintings, textiles, basketwork
and glass, as well as cheese and whisky, are produced locally.

✚ 130 C4 🍽 Excellent cafés in Brodick (£) 🚢 Calmac Ferry from Gourock

BURNS NATIONAL HERITAGE PARK

Best places to see, ➤ 22–23.

CAERLAVEROCK CASTLE AND WILDFOWL AND
WETLANDS TRUST RESERVE

Thirteenth-century **Caerlaverock Castle,** dramatically situated on
the estuary of the River Nith, is the only triangular castle in Britain.
Built of red sandstone, with a double-towered gatehouse, it was
protected by a moat and huge ramparts. The castle was besieged,
damaged and rebuilt by Scottish and English alike, and changed
hands many times, particularly during the Wars of Independence
(1296–1328). Inside there are the remains of a fine Renaissance

mansion house built around 1620. It was finally left a ruin by the depredations of the Covenanters (Scots Protestants) a few years later. Further along the Solway is the **Wildfowl and Wetlands Trust Reserve** where acres of Merseland are conserved to protect the wildlife and to allow visitors to observe from hides. Caerlaverock is home to the most northerly colony of natterjack toads, and every summer the entire Spitsbergen colony of barnacle geese arrives. Activities include listening to the natterjack toads, watching badgers and seeing wild geese take flight.

Caerlaverock Castle

✚ 131 E6 ✉ Near Bankend on B725 13km (8 miles) south of Dumfries ☎ 01387 770244; www.historic-scotland.gov.uk ⏱ Apr–end Sep daily 9.30–6; Oct–end Mar daily 9.30–4.30 👋 Moderate 🍴 Café (£) 🚌 371 from Dumfries

Wildfowl and Wetlands Trust Reserve

☎ 01387 770200; www.wwt.org.uk ⏱ Daily 10–5 👋 Moderate

CULZEAN CASTLE AND COUNTRY PARK

Perched on a cliff top over the Firth of Clyde, Culzean was constructed for the 10th Earl of Cassillis by the architect Robert Adam. After 20 years it was finally finished in 1792. Built in neo-Gothic style, with towers and turrets on the outside, the classical design of the inside is dominated by the majestic oval staircase. During his lifetime, the former US President Dwight D. Eisenhower had the use of the top floor, and his life and work are commemorated in a permanent display. The castle is set in an extensive country park with gardens, seashore, wooded walks and a pond.

✚ 130 D4 ✉ 19km (12 miles) southwest of Ayr on A719 ☎ 01655 884455 ⏱ Castle and Walled Garden Apr–end Oct 10.30–5. Visitor centre Apr–end Oct 9–5.30; Nov–end Mar Sat, Sun 11–4. Park daily 9.30–sunset 👋 Expensive 🍴 Restaurant and coffee shop (£–££) 🚌 60 from Ayr

DUMFRIES

This quiet county town was home to two of Scotland's literary greats, Robert Burns and J. M. Barrie. Robert Burns, after an unsuccessful farming venture at nearby Ellisland, moved to Dumfries and worked as an excise man until his untimely death.

Robert Burns' house is now a museum and on display are the bed he died in and the desk where he penned the words of *Auld Lang Syne*. In the Globe Inn, visitors can sit in the poet's chair but must recite a verse of his poetry or buy the assembled company a drink.

J. M. Barrie attended Dumfries Academy, and it was while playing pirates with his friends in a garden next to the school that Peter Pan was born. The garden was the inspiration for Never Never Land and Captain Hook was his maths teacher. In Dumfries Museum, the earliest example of Barrie's writing can be seen.

✚ 131 E6

Robert Burns House

✉ Burns Street ☎ 01387 255297 ◷ Apr–Sep Mon–Sat 10–5, Sun 2–5; Oct–Mar Tue–Sat 10–1, 2–5 ☝ Free ☎ Several excellent cafés and eateries (£) in town

GALLOWAY FOREST PARK AND GLEN TROOL

The Galloway Forest Park centred around lovely Loch Trool and the Galloway Hills is an area of outstanding natural beauty. Hill-walking in this empty wilderness is rewarded by splendid views over lochs, hills and coast. Less strenuous is a stroll or bicycle through the myriad forest paths or a drive along the Queen's Way to the pretty village of New Galloway. The park's rangers host an extensive calendar of activities throughout the year, from wildlife-spotting walks to special events for children. There is also an excellent mountain bike park in the Kirroughtree area of the forest.

www.forestry.gov.uk/gallowayforestpark

✚ 131 E5 ☎ 01671 402420 🍴 Cafés and tea rooms (£) at various villages and towns throughout the park

KIRKCUDBRIGHT

There is a magical quality to the light in this part of the world that seems to draw artists to the area. The illustrator Jessie M. King and her husband, E. A. Taylor, lived at Green Gate Close on High Street, while Edward Hornel, one of the Glasgow Boys, a group of Scottish painters inspired by the Impressionists, lived nearby at **Broughton House.** Hornel's Georgian mansion, with its Japanese garden, is now a museum to his life and work. In the Old Tolbooth is an art centre featuring the work of local artists. Also worth a visit is the Stewartry Museum and MacLellan's Castle, which dominates the square beside the picturesque working harbour.

✚ 131 E6

Broughton House

✉ High Street ☎ 01557 330437; www.nts.org.uk

🕐 Jul–end Aug daily 12–5; Apr–end Jun, Sep–end Oct Thu–Mon 12–5. Garden only Feb–end Mar Mon–Fri 11–4

👆 Moderate

THE MACHARS

This peninsula south of Newton Stewart is a time warp, reminiscent of Sunday afternoons of yesteryear. Wigtown, once a prosperous and bustling place, used to look and feel like a ghost town. Now, as Scotland's official 'book town', it has a new lease on life and is gradually regaining something of its former glory.

Further south is the sleepy town of Whithorn, where Chrisitianity first came to Scotland with St. Ninian in AD397. Pilgrims flocked here from all over the Christian world until pilgrimage was banned during the Reformation. Much of medieval Whithorn remains, and at the **Whithorn Dig** the earlier settlements are being excavated.

✚ 131 E5

Whithorn Dig

✉ George Street ☎ 01988 500508; www.whithorn.com 🕓 Apr–Oct daily 10.30–5 👋 Inexpensive 🍴 Tea room nearby (£)

NEW ABBEY

Nestling under Criffel, the village of New Abbey is dominated by the ruins of a Cistercian abbey. It was founded in 1273 by Devorgilla de Balliol, wife of the Scottish king

John Balliol, founder of Balliol College, Oxford and became known as **Sweetheart Abbey** because the hearts of Devorgilla and her husband are interred together here.

New Abbey Corn Mill is a water-driven mill, with working machinery. Near New Abbey is the museum of costume and dress at Shambellie House, and at Arbigland, near Kirkbean, is the cottage birthplace of John Paul Jones (1747–92), founder of the US Navy.

If the sky is clear a climb to Criffel's peak, 570m (1,870ft), will provide a view into Scotland, Ireland, England and the Isle of Man.

✚ 131 E6

Sweetheart Abbey

✉ New Abbey ☎ 01387 850397 ⊙ Apr–Sep daily 9.30– 5.30; Oct–Mar Sat–Wed 9.30–4.30 👋 Inexpensive 🍴 Tea room (£) 🚌 372 from Dumfries

New Abbey Corn Mill

✉ New Abbey ☎ 01387 850260; www.historic-scotland.gov.uk ⊙ Apr–Sep daily 9.30–5.30; Oct–Mar Sat–Wed 9.30–4.30 👋 Moderate

NEW LANARK

Best places to see, ➤ 32–33.

SAMYE LING TIBETAN CENTRE

Probably the last thing you would expect to find in this remote and lonely corner of Dumfries and Galloway is a Buddhist monastery. Yet here it is in all its glory. Elaborate oriental buildings in bright red and gold sit high up in the Southern Uplands of Scotland with the tranquil sounds of wind chimes filling the air. Tibetan monks built Samye Ling, but it is home to a community of Buddhists. There are various courses in meditation available, including weekend workshops and retreats, and visitors are very welcome.

www.samyeling.org

✚ 131 D7 ✉ Eskdalemuir ☎ 01387 373232 ⊙ Temple daily until 10pm 👋 Free 🍴 Café on site (£) 🚌 112 from Langholm

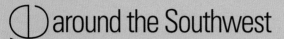# around the Southwest

This drive will take you through some of the finest scenery in Scotland – rugged mountains, rocky coastline, low-lying pastures and picturesque towns and villages.

From Dumfries follow the A710 via New Abbey, Kirkbean (▶ 75) and Colvend to Dalbeattie.

The John Paul Jones birthplace museum near Kirkbean is a tribute to the Scot who founded the American Navy. New Abbey is the site of Sweetheart Abbey (▶ 75).

From Dalbeattie take the A711 to Kirkcudbright, then the A762 to New Galloway.

Tiny Palnackie is the venue for the annual World Flounder Tramping Championships. Here competitors stand in the water, waiting until they feel a flounder moving under their feet, then reach down and scoop up the fish. At Dundrennan is another ruined abbey.

From New Galloway turn right on to the A712 to Balmaclellan, then the B7075 and right onto the A702 to Moniaive.

The clogmaker at Balmaclellan welcomes visitors to his workshop, while the picturesque village of Moniaive has a number of pleasant walks, as well as a good organic café, The Green Tea House.

Take the B729 just beyond Kirkland to Dunscore, then turn right on to a local road heading towards Newtonairds and follow the signs for Shawhead.

At Glenkiln Reservoir, a collection of sculptures by Henry Moore, Jacob Epstein and Auguste Rodin is displayed in the sweeping pastoral landscape. Moore's King and Queen sculpture on the hillside overlooking the reservoir has become the symbol of Glenkiln.

From Glenkiln continue along the side of the reservoir to Shawhead; follow the local road to the A75, turn left and return to Dumfries.

Distance 153km (95 miles)
Time 6–8 hours depending on stops
Start/end point Dumfries ✚ 131 E6
Lunch Craigdarroch Arms

Central Scotland

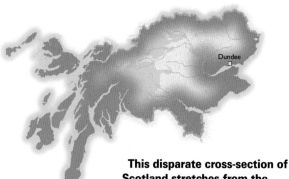

Dundee

This disparate cross-section of Scotland stretches from the lonely island-scattered western coastline of Argyll and the Hebrides to the fishing villages of the East Neuk of Fife on the Firth of Forth, all the way to the silvery Tay, Angus and the featureless expanse of the North Sea beyond. It includes wild hills, moorlands and waterways, the bustling small towns of Scotland's central belt and lush agricultural land.

Rising in the great central plain is Stirling Castle, which saw fierce fighting in the Scottish Wars of Independence (1296–1328), while further north lie the refined country town of Perth, down-to-earth Dundee and the heather-covered Angus Glens.

DUNDEE

Dundee straggles untidily along the River Tay, its two distinctive bridges reaching out long thin highways of road and rail over the broad stretch of water to Fife. Of the three Js – jute, jam and journalism – which were the lifeblood of the town, only journalism remains, in the shape of D. C. Thomson, who publish the *Dandy* and *Beano* comics and the *Sunday Post*. In the surrounding countryside, the berry fields that supplied the jam factories now allow you to pick your own fruit. The town has reinvented itself as a popular conference venue, helped by the unassuming friendliness of the people. This, together with the unpretentious cultural life, excellent museums, including the interactive Sensation Science Centre, and small theatres, make it an agreeable base for touring the area.

✛ 131 A7

Broughty Ferry and Castle

Broughty Ferry, once a separate village, is now a suburb of Dundee. It is popular with Dundonians and visitors alike, with its eclectic mix of restaurants, pubs and shops and sandy beach along the banks of the Tay. Fifteenth-century **Broughty Castle,** now a museum, tells the story of Broughty Ferry and the whaling industry.

Broughty Castle

☎ 01382 436916 ◷ Mon–Sat 10–4, Sun 12.30–4; closed Mon Oct–Mar ♨ Free

RRS *Discovery* and HM Frigate *Unicorn*

Once the pride of the Panmuir yard, where it was built in 1901 for the polar expeditions of Captain Robert Falcon Scott, the **Royal Research Ship *Discovery*** lay rotting for years on London's Thames Embankment. Finally, the ship was restored and returned to its birthplace. Now housed at the specially-designed Discovery Point, it has become a major tourist attraction.

The Frigate *Unicorn*, further along the Tay at Victoria Dock, is the oldest British warship still afloat. Built in 1824, it was, incredibly, still in service until 1968.

RRS *Discovery*

✉ Victoria Quay, near the Tay Bridge

☎ 01382 201245; www.rrsdiscovery.com

🕐 Apr–end Oct Mon–Sat 10–6, Sun 11–6; Nov–end Mar Mon–Sat 10–5, Sun 11–5 👋 Expensive 🍴 Café (£)

McManus Art Gallery and Museum

This is a gem of a place, one of the finest Victorian buildings in Dundee, and that's just the outside. Indoors, the museum covers Dundee's history from the ancient Picts to modern times. There's also a great display on the Tay Bridge disaster. On 28 December 1879, the bridge collapsed in a storm after only 18 months, and 75 people died. Upstairs in the Albert Hall, with its pitch pine-panelled roof, are collections of glass, gold, silver, musical instruments and furniture, including the table where death warrants for captured Jacobites were signed after the Battle of Culloden in 1746. The Victoria Gallery has Scottish collections and superb Pre-Raphaelites.

www.mcmanus.co.uk

✉ Albert Square ☎ 01382 432350 🕐 Closed for renovation at the time of writing; expected to reopen in late summer of 2008 🖐 Free 🍴 Café (£)

Mills Observatory

This is the only full-time public observatory in Britain, and offers guided tours. There are special openings for eclipses and the odd visiting comet. Winter evenings are the best time to go, but in the summer, when it's light, there are good exhibits and displays.
www.dundeecity.gov.uk/mills

✉ Balgay Park. Approach via Perth Road, Blackness Avenue, Balgay Road
☎ 01382 435967 🕐 Apr–end Sep Tue–Fri 11–5, Sat, Sun 12.30–4; Oct–end Mar Mon–Fri 4pm–10pm, Sat, Sun 12.30–4

🖐 Free 🍴 Light refreshments (£)
❓ Reservations essential for large groups and for Planetarium

Verdant Works

Verdant Works was one of Dundee's many jute mills that produced hessian and sacking, and once employed 50,000 people locally; it has been restored and reconstructed as a museum. Volunteers operate textile machines, while 'Juteopolis', a 15-minute film, explains the impact of the industry on the city and its people. Every day at 1pm the works' 'bummer' (whistle) is blown, a sound that marked the livelihood of many families and recalls its history in an evocative way.
www.verdantworks.com

✉ 27 West Henderson's Wynd ☎ 01382 225282 🖐 Apr–end Oct Mon–Sat 10–5, Sun 11–6; Nov–end Mar Wed–Sat 10.30–4.30, Sun 11–4.30 🖐 Expensive 🍴 Refreshments (£)

a drive around Central Scotland

Start from Perth. Take the A85, then turn right onto the A93 and right again onto the A94. (Scone Palace ► 95 is 2.5km/1.5 miles further along the A93.) At Balbeggie, take the B953 to Inchture, then turn left on to the A90. Take the A85 left through Dundee, past Discovery Point and follow the signs for the Tay Bridge and the A92. Pass through Newport-on-Tay and Leuchars to St. Andrews, then follow the A917. Follow the coastline of the East Neuk, diverting through the picturesque villages of Crail, Anstruther, Pittenweem, St. Monance and Elie.

From Crail take the B940 to Scotland's Secret Bunker. This underground relic of the Cold War would have become the administrative centre of Scotland in the event of a nuclear attack. It was an official secret until 1994 when it opened to the public. Part of it is still operational.

Turn left on to the A915.

Have a look at Lower Largo, with its statue of Alexander Selkirk, the prototype of Robinson Crusoe. A native of Largo, Selkirk ran away to sea and was marooned on Juan Fernand Island from 1705 to 1709.

Continue on the A91, then turn right on to the A911 and in Glenrothes turn right on to the A92, then left on to the A912. At Falkland follow the B936 to Auchtermuchty and turn left on to the A91. From the A91 turn left on to the B919, left on to the A911, then after Kinnesswood, right on to the B920. At the intersection turn right on to the

B9097, right again on to the B996 and continue to Kinross.

This route circles Loch Leven with the 14th-century ruins of Loch Leven Castle on an island. Mary, Queen of Scots, was imprisoned here in 1567.

Take the A922 to Milnathort and the B996 via Glenfarg to the A912. Turn left and follow the road through Bridge of Earn back to Perth.

Distance 190km (118 miles)
Time 6–8 hours including stops
Start/end point Perth ✚ 131 A7
Lunch The Naafi at the Secret Bunker (£) ☎ 01333 310301

More to see in Central Scotland

THE ANGUS GLENS

The Glens of Angus are a series of five glorious glens, rich in flora and fauna. Of particular interest are the red deer and Arctic plants. Glen Clova is the most picturesque of the Glens, offering several lovely walks. Jock's Road, leading through the mountains to Braemar, some 22.5km (14 miles) away, is spectacular. The path clings, precariously at times, to the hill's edge, the water runs far below and, as you climb, the view of the glen behind falls away in a changing, winding perspective, misty in the distance. Beware, this is passable only in summer.

✚ 135 F8

BO'NESS AND KINNEIL RAILWAY

This is one of the best small independent railway lines and the largest collection of vintage trains in Scotland. The track from Bo'ness leads 5km/3 miles to Birkhill, where you can visit the Birkhill Clay Mine or stroll in the Avon Gorge before the old steam train departs for the return trip.

www.srps.org.uk

✚ 131 B6 ✉ Off Union Street, Bo'ness
☎ 01506 822298 🕑 Apr–Oct every weekend
(Jul–Aug Tue–Sun); Santa Specials Dec
weekends 🕑 Moderate

CRARAE GARDEN

Between Inveraray and Lochgilphead, this National Trust garden is
laid out around the glen of the Crarae Burn that flows into Loch
Fyne. Covering around 25ha (62 acres), there are two walking
routes, the inner and outer circles that both start from the car park.
Strategically placed seats allow you to enjoy majestic views over
Loch Fyne while admiring the snowdrops, daffodils, bluebells,
azaleas, rhododendrons or magnolias, depending on the season.
www.nts.org.uk

✚ 130 B4 ✉ A83, 16km (10 miles) southwest of Inveraray ☎ 01546 886614
🕑 Gardens daily dawn–dusk; visitor centre Apr–Oct daily 10–5 🕑 Moderate
🍴 Refreshments (£)

CULROSS AND CULROSS PALACE

The National Trust for Scotland tends the red-tiled houses and
whitewashed walls of this delightful town. Walk through the
cobbled Back Causeway, visit the remains of the Cistercian
Culross Abbey, or the Study, a restored 17th-century house.
The 16th-century merchant's house known as **Culross Palace**
is the main attraction, with little rooms and narrow passages.
St. Mungo, the founder, and
patron saint of Glasgow, was
reputedly born here.

✚ 131 B6 ✉ 12km (7.5 miles) west
of Dunfermline
Culross Palace
☎ 01383 880359; www.nts.org.uk
🕓 Apr–Sep daily 12–5 🕑 Moderate
🍴 Café (£)

EAST NEUK OF FIFE

The coastline of the East Neuk is dotted with a string of little fishing villages. Quaint cottages with red-tiled roofs and crow-stepped gables perch around secluded harbours. Crail is the prettiest, while Anstruther and Pittenweem are regular working ports. Anstruther is home to the **Scottish Fisheries Museum,** where the entire history of fishing in Scotland unfolds. Kellie Castle, north of Anstruther, is a restored 16th-century building with

a garden full of nooks and crannies.

➕ 131 A8

Scottish Fisheries Museum

✉ Anstruther Harbour

☎ 01333 310628; www.scottishfishmuseum.org

🕐 Apr–end Sep Mon–Sat 10–5.30, Sun 11–5; Oct–end Mar Mon–Sat 10–4.30, Sun 12–4.30

♿ Moderate

🍴 Tea room (£)

THE FALKIRK WHEEL

Designed to connect the Forth and Clyde and Union canals, this massive rotating boat lift carries eight boats at a time. The state-of-the-art visitor centre tells the story of the Wheel and the history of canals. Boat trips from the centre sail on to the Wheel that ascends to join the Union Canal 35m (115ft) above. The journey continues along the canal by the Antonine Wall before returning.

www.thefalkirkwheel.co.uk

➕ 131 B6 ✉ Lime Road, Tamfourhill, Falkirk ☎ 01324 619888 🕐 Visitor centre Feb–end Mar Mon–Fri 10–4.30, Sat, Sun 10–6; Apr–end Oct daily 9.30–6 ♿ Visitor centre free; boat trip expensive

HELENSBURGH AND HILL HOUSE

The main attraction in this attractive Georgian town on the Firth of Clyde is **Hill House,** designed by Charles Rennie Mackintosh in 1902 for the publisher Walter Blackie. Mackintosh was given a completely free hand in the design of the house, its interior and furnishings. The result is one of the finest art nouveau houses in Britain, now painstakingly restored by the National Trust for Scotland. The exterior echoes a traditional tower with its irregular windows, round turret and solid expanses of wall. Inside, it is light and elegant with perfect proportions and delightful glimpses of the adjoining spaces as you move through it.

Henry Bell, the inventor of the *Comet,* an early steam-driven boat, was swimming instructor in Helensburgh, which was also the birthplace of the inventor of television, John Logie Baird.

✚ 131 B5

Hill House

✉ Upper Colquhoun Street ☎ 01436 673900; www.nts.org.uk ⏱ Apr–Oct daily 1.30–5.30 ♿ Expensive 🍴 Tea room (£)

THE INNER HEBRIDES

There's a magical quality about the islands of Islay, Jura, Mull, Iona, Coll and Tiree. Most tourists head for Tobermory on Mull, with its bright houses fronting the harbour where, tradition has it, the wreck of a Spanish galleon lies laden with gold. Iona, with its mighty cathedral and connections with St. Columba, draws pilgrims from all over the world. Jura has wonderful, blindingly white, sandy beaches that are all but deserted – just the spot to get away from it all. But it is to Islay that you must go if you want to experience some of the finest whiskies in Scotland. Islay malts are unique and easily distinguished by their smokey, peaty taste.

➕ 134 F2

INVERARAY

This small 18th-century town, built by the Duke of Argyll, clan chief of the Campbells, has an enchanting view over Loch Fyne. The old gaol and adjoining courthouse are now a museum. Inveraray Castle, home of the Duke of Argyll, would not

be out of place on the Loire. In the stable block the Combined Operations Museum is dedicated to the troops that trained on Loch Fyne for the D-Day landings in Normandy. Inside the castle itself is a collection of weapons given to the Campbells by the government to help repress the Jacobites.

Southwest of Inveraray is the restored township of **Auchindrain,** now a folk museum, with around 20 thatched cottages set up to re-create life prior to the Clearances.

✚ 130 A4

Auchindrain

✉ 10km (6 miles) southwest of Inveraray ☎ 01499 500235; www.auchindrainmuseum.org.uk ◷ Apr–Oct daily 10–5 ⚑ Moderate

KIRRIEMUIR

Kirriemuir was the birthplace of J. M. Barrie, novelist, dramatist and creator of *Peter Pan.* The house he was born in is a **museum,** and outside is the wash house: the prototype of the house the Lost Boys built for Wendy, which the young Barrie used as a theatre for his first plays. Barrie is buried in the local cemetery.

✚ 135 F8

JM Barrie's Birthplace

✉ 9 Brechin Road ☎ 01575 572646; www.nts.org.uk ◷ Jul–end Aug daily 12–5; Apr–end Jun, Sep–Oct Fri–Wed 12–5 ⚑ Moderate

LINLITHGOW

Mary, Queen of Scots, was born here at **Linlithgow Palace** in 1542. Although a royal building had existed here since the time of David I (1124–53), it was James I who built the present one. It survived until 1746 when it was destroyed by fire, but it's well worth a visit. Overlooking Linlithgow Loch, the roofless ruin has spiral staircases, stately rooms, a magnificent Great Hall, and a brewery down below.

✚ 131 B6

Linlithgow Palace

✉ South shore of loch ☎ 01506 842896; www.historic-scotland.gov.uk
⊙ Apr–Sep daily 9.30–5.30; Oct–Mar Mon–Sun 9.30–4.30 👆 Moderate

LOCH AWE

This is the longest freshwater loch in Scotland. There are forest walks at Barnaline, near Dalavich, and near the head of the loch you will find the tiny island of Inishail, with its 13th-century chapel. At Taynuilt, visit the restored industrial heritage centre of **Bonawe Iron Furnace** before heading back towards the loch via the gloomy Pass of Brander for a tour of the Cruachan Power Station. The

station is built into Ben Cruachan, where hydroelectricity is generated by water pumped up the mountain from the loch below. **www.**historic-scotland.gov.uk

✚ 130 A4

Bonawe Iron Furnace

✉ Off the A85 at Bonawe ☎ 01866 822432 🕐 Mar–end Sep daily 9.30–5.30 ✋ Moderate

LOCH LOMOND

Loch Lomond and the Trossachs together form a National Park. The loch can be overcrowded during the tourist season, but it is a great beauty spot. To escape the crowds, take one of the boat trips from Balloch that go round the small islands on the loch, or follow the West Highland Way on the east bank to Rowardennan and Balmaha. From here, a path to climbs up Ben Lomond, 972m (3,188ft), with views from the top across the Southern Highlands. **www.**visitscottishheartlands.com

✚ 131 B5 🛈 National Park Gateway Centre ✉ Ben Lomond Way, Loch Lomond Shores, Balloch ☎ 08707 200631 🕐 Aug daily 9–6.30; Sep 10–6; Oct, Apr–May 10–5.30; Nov–Mar 10–5, Jun 9.30–6

MONTROSE BASIN WILDLIFE CENTRE

The Basin, a huge tidal lagoon of mud, is a rich habitat for all manner of wildlife. Humans may hold their noses but to the geese, waders and swans that frequent the basin, grubbing in the smelly mud is a gourmet experience. Telescopes, video cameras and binoculars are strategically placed to enable visitors to watch without disturbing the birds, and there is a series of guided walks led by the resident ranger.

www.swt.org.uk

✚ 137 F5 ✉ 1.5km (1 mile) from Montrose, on the A92 ☎ 01674 676336 ⏱ Reserve summer 8–8, winter dawn–dusk. Visitor centre 15 Mar–15 Nov daily 10–5; Nov–15 Mar Fri–Sun 10.30–4 ✋ Inexpensive

OBAN

Oban, the main terminal for Caledonian MacBrayne Ferries, is known as the gateway to the Isles. McCaig's Folly, a granite tower, was built for no real reason on a hill overlooking the town. However, it looks dramatic, particularly when floodlit at night. Outside the town are the ruins of 13th-century **Dunstaffnage Castle,** where Flora MacDonald was imprisoned after helping Bonnie Prince Charlie in his escape. The Isle of Kerrera in Oban Bay, with a population of less than 50, is easily reached by ferry. It is a peaceful retreat with great views over to Mull and Jura.

✚ 130 A4

Dunstaffnage Castle

✉ 5km (3 miles) north of Oban, off the A85

☎ 01631 562465; www.historic-scotland.gov.uk

🕐 Apr–end Sep daily 9.30–5.30 (4.30 Oct);
Nov–end Mar Sat–Wed 9.30–4.30 ✋ Inexpensive

PERTH

Perth is a prosperous market town in the heart of rich farmlands. Visit the Victorian water-driven oat mill at Lower City Mills and the cobbled streets around it. Bell's Cherrybank Gardens has Britain's largest collection of heathers and a super children's play area. At the Caithness Glass factory see glass blown in the traditional way.

Scone, just to the north, where all the monarchs of Scotland were crowned on the Stone of Destiny, is the historic heart of Scotland. Ancient **Scone Palace** was restored and extended in the 19th century and this elegant Gothic mansion is home to the Earl of Mansfield. The grounds, house and history are fascinating, but there is also an extraordinary collection of furniture, porcelain, delicate ivories, and papier mâché that once belonged to Louis XV of France.

✚ 131 A7

Scone Palace

✉ Off the A93 Braemar Road, 3km (2 miles) northeast of Perth ☎ 01738 552300 🕐 Apr–end Oct 9.30–5.30; last admission 5; grounds open until 5.45 ✋ Expensive 🍴 Restaurant (££) and coffee shop (£)

PITLOCHRY

Pitlochry is a popular tourist town on the banks of the River Tummel, where the Blair Athol Distillery has been making its famous malt since 1798. The power station produces electricity from the artificially created Loch Faskally, and the salmon ladder to help the fish negotiate the dam is a sight not to be missed. Pitlochry Festival Theatre is famous for its productions. Enjoy a backstage tour during the day and return in the evening for a performance of the latest play.

Near the town is the **Pass of Killiecrankie,** site of the famous Battle of Killicrankie in 1689 where the Jacobites, led by Graham of Claverhouse (Bonnie Dundee), defeated the government forces, although Dundee himself was killed. This deep wooded gorge has a visitor centre with exhibits on the gorge and the battle.

➕ 135 F7

Pass of Killiecrankie

✉ Off the A9, 5km (3 miles) north of Pitlochry ☎ 01796 473233; wwwnts.org.uk ⊕ Site open all year. Visitor centre Apr–end Oct daily 10–5.30 ⬚ Free 🍴 Snack bar (£)

ST. ANDREWS

Scotland's oldest university town is world famous as the home of golf, which has been played here since the 15th century. The Royal and Ancient Golf Club is the governing body of the sport and in 1873 the first British Open Championship was held here. The **British Golf Museum** is the best there is, with lots of hands-on stuff and plenty

of history. However, if golf is not your scene take a walk around the historic streets to the great cathedral, once the largest in Scotland. It was consecrated in 1318 in the presence of King Robert the Bruce and destroyed in 1559 by supporters of John Knox. An impressive ruin, it is particularly beautiful at twilight in half silhouette.

✚ 131 A8

British Golf Museum

✉ Bruce Embankment, opposite the Royal and Ancient Golf Club ☎ 01334 460046; www. britishgolfmuseum.co.uk ⏱ Apr–end Oct daily 9.30–5.30, Sun 10–5; Nov–end Mar daily 10–4 💷 Moderate

STIRLING

Stirling Castle, like Edinburgh Castle, is perched atop the plug of an extinct volcano, but in many ways Stirling is more dramatic. Surrounded by a wide plain, the castle is the most prominent sight for miles around and in past times the narrow bridge here was a strategic gateway between North and South. Many of the decisive battles in Scotland's history, including Stirling Bridge (1297) and Bannockburn (1314) were fought around here. At the Lady's Rock in the cemetery there is a pointer to all the surrounding battle sites. Bannockburn's visitor centre details the battle in an excellent audiovisual presentation. The Wallace Monument high on the cliffs overlooking the site of the Battle of Stirling Bridge contains the hero's massive two-handed sword.

✚ 131 B6
Stirling Castle
✉ Castle Wynd ☎ 01786 431316 ⏰ Apr–end Sep
daily 9.30–6; Oct–end Mar daily 9.30–5 👆 Expensive
🍴 Café (£)

THE TROSSACHS NATIONAL PARK

Together with Loch Lomond (➤ 93), the
Trossachs form Scotland's first National Park.
This wild countryside of moors, hills and
forests, from Loch Katrine to Loch Lomond,
was the haunt of Rob Roy MacGregor – outlaw,
cattle thief, murderer or hero depending on
your point of view. He died at a ripe old age in
his own bed and is buried in the beautiful
churchyard at Balquhidder. The Trossachs is the
largest area of wilderness in central Scotland,
with excellent walking, climbing and fishing and
the spectacular scenery. If you can't make it to
the Highlands, this is as near as you'll get to the

majestic scale of the north. Its
position right at the heart of
Scotland means that it is easily
accessible and very popuar.

Main towns in the area are
Callander and Aberfoyle.
www.lochlomond-trossachs.org
✚ 131 A5 🛈 Trossachs Discovery
Centre ✉ Main Street, Aberfoyle
☎ 08707 200604;
www.visitscottishheartlands.com
⏰ Daily Apr–Oct, Sat–Sun
Nov–Mar. Many tourist information
offices; check website for closest

The North

The Highlands and Islands are the Scotland of literature, romance and the movies, a vast area, much of it unforgiving mountain or natural moorland.

Aberdeen

Many species of wildlife that have disappeared elsewhere survive in the scarcely populated wildernesses here. Scattered ruined cottages remain, testimony to a more populous past before the Clearances in the 18th and 19th centuries, when the landlords drove the people from the land in favour of more profitable sheep.

Highlanders emigrated in droves to the New World, taking with them their oral traditions of music and storytelling and their memories of the land they left behind. Exiled Scots and their descendants get very nostalgic at the mention of misty glens, heather-covered hillsides and dark deep lochs. It is easy to mock, but travel this land once and you will understand how they feel.

ABERDEEN

Aberdeen, the grey granite city of the North, is the hub of
Scotland's oil industry, a thriving fishing port and home to one
of the four ancient universities of Scotland. Surprisingly, for the
most northerly city of Scotland, it is famed for its imaginative and
prolific gardens. The nightlife is lively on account of the university
and the prosperity of its cosmopolitan population. Understanding
the language, however, can present problems and a crash course
in the Doric, the local dialect, might be a good idea. In the
meantime, to the standard greeting of 'Fit like?', simply answer
'Nae bad, foo's yersel?' Translated it means 'How are you?', 'Not
bad, how are you?'

137 E6

Aberdeen Maritime Museum

The 1593 Provost Ross's house, one of the oldest buildings in the
city, is home to this remarkable museum that tells the story of
Aberdeen's maritime heritage. Everything is covered, from herring
fishing and whaling to ship-building and the late 20th-century oil
industry. The ancient rooms combine with state-of-the-art

computers, audiovisual technology, objects and oral history.
www.aagm.co.uk

✉ Shiprow ☎ 01224 337700 ⏰ Daily 10–5 (12–3 Sun) ✋ Moderate

Fish Market and Harbour

Fishing is still one of the mainstays of the local economy and few
sights can compare with the bustling harbour where fishing
vessels lie alongside oil-rig supply boats and modern cruise liners.
Pay an early morning visit to the fish market to mingle with the
buyers and fishermen as thousands of tons of freshly landed fish
are bid for then loaded into huge refrigerated trucks to be
transported throughout the UK.

Provost Skene's House

Dating from 1545, Aberdeen's
oldest private dwelling house
was the home of its provost
(mayor), Sir George Skene, from
1676 to 1685, and is preserved
almost unchanged. Astonishingly,
its luminous religious paintings
survived Reformation zeal to
obliterate Roman Catholic
imagery, and years of neglect.
Finally, as a slum threatened with
demolition, it was saved to
become a museum in 1953. It
provides a faithful representation
of life for the comfortable
burghers of Aberdeen in the
late 17th century.

✉ 45 Guestrow, off Broad Street
☎ 01224 641086 ⏰ Mon–Sat 10–5,
Sun 1–4 ✋ Free 🍴 Café (£)

Satrosphere Science Centre

This is the only permanent interactive exhibition of Science and Technology in Scotland and a great place to take children. There are no 'do not touch' signs here; visitors are actively encouraged to touch, look and feel. About 80 of the 150 exhibits and experiments are on display at any one time. You can find out about the geological formation of northeast Scotland, marvel at the industry and organization inside a beehive then compare it with a colony of ants, guess what the mystery sticky liquids are, test the speed of your reactions, experience the Satrosphere's very own black hole and much, much more. Fascinating for visitors of all ages, it may trigger a lifelong interest in science.

www.satrosphere.net

✉ The Tram Sheds, 179 Constitution Street ☎ 01224 640340
🕐 Daily 10–5 💹 Moderate

Tolbooth Museum

The Tolbooth Museum, within the granite Town House, was the town gaol in 17th-century Aberdeen. The narrow staircases and cramped cells chillingly evoke the grim existence of prisoners here. An audiovisual display and a lifelike model of a prisoner tell tales of the wretched life and of escapes from the bleak conditions.

✉ Castle Street ☎ 01224 621167/01569 766073 🕐 Apr–Oct Wed–Mon 1.30–4.30 💹 Free

More to see in the North

BALLATER AND BALMORAL

Balmoral, a fine example of Scottish Baronial architecture, was converted to a private residence for Queen Victoria in 1855 and became a well-loved summer residence for the Royal Family. The local shops

in Ballater flaunt their 'By Royal Appointment' signs. The town is a grand base for exploring the area, and Balmoral Estate hires out ponies.

www.balmoralcastle.com

➕ 136 E4 ✉ Balmoral Estate: 13km (8 miles) west of Ballater on the A93 ☎ 013397 42534 🕐 Apr–Aug daily 10–5. Winter gardens by guided tour only 👋 Moderate 🍴 Café (£)

BETTYHILL

This tiny coastal village, at the heart of the crofting community, suffered mass emigration during the Highland Clearances. Tiny **Strathnaver Museum** tells the story of some of the most horrific evictions, ordered by the Countess of Sutherland. Ironically the village was named after her. Nearby are two of the whitest sand beaches in Britain and the Invernaver Nature Reserve, where otters and Arctic terns can often be spotted.

✚ 136 A3

Strathnaver Museum

✉ Clachan, Bettyhill ☎ 01641 521418; www.strathnavermuseum.org.uk ⏰ Apr–end Oct Mon–Sat 10–1, 2–5 (and by arrangement) ✋ Inexpensive

THE CAIRNGORMS

Within the area of these mountains, outdoor enthusiasts can find skiing, canoeing, mountaineering, bicycling and walking and a rich variety of flora and fauna. The 40km (25 miles) of the Lairig Ghru, running through a majestic mountain pass from Aviemore to Braemar, are reputed to be the best walk in Scotland, although its unpredictable weather and biting cold can test the endurance of the

most experienced walker. However, there are lots of shorter, less demanding walks in this glorious landscape. Aviemore village is ideal for exploring the area and its

numerous shops sell and rent equipment. Loch Morlich Watersports and the Scottish National Sports Council's Glenmore Lodge provide facilities and training.
www.cairngorms.co.uk

➕ 136 E4 🛈 Grampian Road, Aviemore ☎ 01479 810363 🕒 Mon–Fri 8–8, Sat 9–5.30, Sun 10–4

CALEDONIAN CANAL AND THE GREAT GLEN

One of Thomas Telford's greatest engineering achievements was the Caledonian Canal linking lochs Ness, Oich, Lochy and Linnhe from Inverness in the east to Fort William in the west. A slow boat through the Great Glen, watching the reflection of forest greenery or massed broom along the banks, is a tranquil and awesome experience. For the more energetic there are lots of off-road walking or bicycling trails on disused military roads, the old rail line or the towpath. At Fort Augustus, the **Clansmen's Centre** illustrates 17th-century clan life in a reconstructed turf house.

➕ 136 E2

Clansmen's Centre

✉ On the banks of the canal in Fort Augustus ☎ 01320 366444 🕒 Apr–end Oct daily 10–6.30 ✋ Inexpensive

CROMARTY

Cromarty is a picturesque village on the northeast
coast of the Black Isle. The local museum in the
old **courthouse** and the thatched cottage of Hugh
Miller's birthplace bring the varied past of this little
port to life. Take a boat trip to watch dolphins, porpoises and the
occasional killer whale. The massive oil rigs of Nigg and Invergordon
dominate the Cromarty Firth by day and light up the night.

✚ 136 C3

Cromarty Courthouse

✉ Church Street ☎ 01381 600418; www.cromarty-courthouse.org.uk
🕒 Apr–end Oct daily 10–5 💷 Moderate

CULLODEN BATTLEFIELD

Best places to see, ➤ 26–27.

DORNOCH

In 1722, Dornoch was the last place in Scotland to burn a witch.
To the south of the town square, the Witch's Stone is a reminder of
the poor soul who was roasted in a barrel of tar for allegedly turning
her daughter into a pony. The focal point of the square is the tiny
cathedral. All but destroyed in the 16th century and rebuilt in the
19th century, it houses an eerie collection of skulls and coffins.

✚ 136 C3 ℹ The Square ☎ 01862 810400 🕒 All year

FORT GEORGE

After the rout of Bonnie Prince Charlie's Highland army at Culloden
in 1746, the Hanoverians embarked on a drastic plan to subdue the
'rebellious Scots'. One measure was the construction of Fort George,
on a spit running into the Moray Firth. It is still home of the
Regimental Museum of the Queen's Own Highlanders.

✚ 136 D3 ✉ Ardersier, B9039, off the A96 west of Nairn ☎ 01667 462777
🕒 Apr–end Sep daily 9.30–6; Oct–end Mar Mon–Sat 9.30–4.30, Sun 9.30–6.30
💷 Moderate 🍴 Tea room (£)

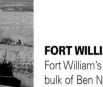

FORT WILLIAM

Fort William's location, at the foot of the Great Glen and with the bulk of Ben Nevis to the east, makes it a popular area for walkers and mountaineers. It marks the end of the West Highland Way, which runs for 152km (95 miles) from the outskirts of Glasgow to Fort William. This is the most popular long-distance walk in Scotland and is broken down into seven daily sections; the final stretch brings you into Fort William with its pubs and restaurants.

The **Nevis Range Mountain Experience,** north of Fort William, offers a lift most of the way up Aonach Mor (a neighbour of Ben Nevis) in a gondola. The 650-m trip is popular with climbers, walkers, cyclists and, if the weather is right, skiers.

✚ 135 F5 🚹 Cameron Centre, Cameron Square ☎ 01397 703781

Nevis Range Mountain Experience

✉ Off A82, 11km (7 miles) north of Fort William ☎ 01397 705825; www.nevisrange.co.uk ⊕ 19 Dec–12 Nov daily 10–5 (Winter 9–5; Jul 9–6) ✋ Expensive

GLEN AFFRIC

As well as having some of the most serious walking, Glen Affric is undoubtedly one of the most beautiful glens in Scotland, with stretches of lovely lochs and forestry. The abundance of birch, pine and alder that grace the glen is a glorious sight in blazing autumn hues. It has one of the most remote youth hostels in Britain, requiring a hike of several miles to reach it.

✚ 135 E5 ✉ Southwest of Cannich, off the A831

GLEN COE

Best places to see, ➤ 30–31.

INVEREWE GARDENS

The Gulf Stream flows around the west coast of Scotland producing a warm temperate climate, ideal for gardens. Inverewe was created between 1862 and 1922 by the estate owner,

Osgood Mackenzie. The garden has spilled out from its original walled enclave to cover the peninsula. Scots pine, birch, oak and rowan stand alongside semi-tropical exotic plants in a series of small gardens.
www.nts.org.uk

➕ 134 C4 ✉ Poolewe ☎ 01445 781200
🕐 Easter–end Oct daily 9–9; Nov–Easter daily 9.30–5 👆 Expensive 🍽 Restaurant (£)

INVERNESS

Inverness is an attractive town, built mainly in the 19th century, with a fine cathedral and castle. Situated on the Moray Firth at the eastern end of the Caledonian Canal, it is the largest town in the Highlands, a transport hub and the best base for exploring.

➕ 136 D3 ℹ Castle Wynd ☎ 01463 234353 🕐 All year

KINGUSSIE

Kingussie, a typical small town built around a single main street, is an oasis of tranquillity bypassed by the hurly-burly of the main artery north, the A9. At the **Highland Folk Museum** you can explore reconstructions of a Lewis black house (a traditional Hebridean low stone dwelling with thatched roof), a salmon smoking shed and a water mill, as well as finding out everything there is to know about the history of the area. Nearby the ruins of Ruthven Barracks stand proud and roofless against the skyline. They were part of the fortifications built to ensure stability in the region after the Jacobite Rebellion of 1745. From Ruthven you can walk a surviving stretch of General Wade's military road, crossing a perfectly preserved example of a Wade bridge near Dalwhinnie.

➕ 136 E3

Highland Folk Museum

✉ Duke Street ☎ 01540 661307 🕐 Apr–Aug Mon–Sun 10.30–5.30; Sep–Oct Mon–Fri 9.30–4.30; Nov–Mar groups by appointment 👆 Moderate

LOCH NESS

The world-famous loch is forever linked to its resident beastie, the Loch Ness Monster. The loch is long and deep and swarming with Nessie spotters. At Drumnadrochit there are two monster exhibitions: the Original Loch Ness Monster Exhibition, and the considerably better **Loch Ness 2000 Exhibition Centre.**

Castle Urquhart, a couple of miles south, is the best monster spotting site, where most of the Nessie photographs have been taken. The ruins of the 14th-century castle themselves are worth a visit. Perched atop a rocky cliff the castle was of strategic importance in guarding the Great Glen. It was destroyed in 1692 to prevent its use by the Jacobites.

✛ 136 D2

Loch Ness 2000 Exhibition Centre

✉ Drumnadrochit ☎ 01456 450573; www.loch-ness-scotland.com ◑ Jul, Aug daily 9–8; Easter–end May daily 9.30–5; Jun, Sep daily 9–6, Oct daily 9.30–5.30; Nov–Easter daily 10–3.30 ✋ Moderate

ROTHIEMURCHUS

The huge estate of Rothiemurchus, belonging to the Grant family, extends from the village of Aviemore to the Cairngorm plateaus. The lovely woodlands here, with the Cairngorms forming a backdrop, are particularly noted for their magnificent Caledonian pine. From the estate visitor centre, there's access to a superb mountain bicycle track and miles of footpaths through forests, over heather moorlands and by lochs and rivers. There is also a nature trail around Loch an Eilean and other activities include clay-pigeon shooting, ranger walks and fishing on the Spey.

www.rothiemurchus.net

✚ 136 E3

✉ 1.5km (1 mile) southeast from Aviemore on the Ski Road ☎ 01479 812345

⦿ Daily 9.30–5.30 🖐 Free; various charges for different activities

🍴 Restaurant, coffee shop (£–££)

SHETLAND AND ORKNEY

These islands were formerly Norwegian, and the Norse influence is evident in language and customs. Orkney is a few miles off the mainland, while Shetland is 96km (60 miles) further north. Each one is a scattering of islands, abounding in wildlife, particularly sea birds. In both, the Mainland refers to the main island while the rest of Scotland is known as 'The Sooth'.

🛈 Shetland Island Tourism, Market Cross ☎ 01595 693434

🛈 Orkney Tourist Board, 6 Broad Street, Kirkwall ☎ 01856 872001

SHETLAND
Foula

About 22km (14 miles) east of the Mainland is Foula. Traces of an ancient way of life – peat fires and eking out a living – cling to this remote island. Until a few years ago, the island schoolteacher was responsible for christenings, marriages and funerals in his role as Church of Scotland missionary. Foula teems with birds, particularly puffins and great skuas.

✚ 138 C3 🚢 Ferries to Foula from Walls ☎ 07881 823732 for times

Jarlshof

This ancient settlement was inhabited from the Stone Age to the 17th century. There's a broch (round tower of two layers of stones with stairs built into the thickness of the wall) and a medieval building, but the most interesting dwellings are the Norse longhouses and the complex wheelhouse structures with underground corridors, bedrooms and central hearths.

✚ 138 C3 ✉ Sumburgh ☎ 01950 460112 🕒 Apr–Sep daily 9.30–6.30 👋 Inexpensive

Lerwick

On Lerwick's attractive waterfront fishing boats jostle along-side oil industry transporters and the Greenpeace *Rainbow*

Warrior, a frequent visitor. The narrow main street runs behind the harbour and countless tiny alleys climb up the hill.

Up Helly Aa, once a pagan fire festival to celebrate the end of the ancient Yule celebration, is now a well organized spectacle in which a thousand men with blazing torches march through the streets of Lerwick. Behind them they drag a Viking galley to the burning ground where they throw their torches into the vessel. If you can't be there to see it in January there is an excellent exhibition with an audiovisual with examples of Viking costumes and pictures of bearded warriors in winged helmets, standing before the burning craft.

✚ 138 C4

Up Helly Aa Exhibition

✉ Galley Shed, off Sunniva Street 🕐 Mid-May to mid-Sep, Tue 2–4, 7–9, Fri 7–9, Sat 2–4 ✋ Inexpensive

ORKNEY

Italian Chapel

Although built from Nissen huts, concrete, barbed wire and paint by Italian POWs in 1943, the love and reverence that went into this exquisite little gem are evident. Artist Domenico Chiocchetti designed the interior, creating *trompe-l'oeil* stonework and windows, and a magnificent fresco altarpiece.

✚ 138 E2 ✉ Lamb Holm ⏰ Apr–end Sep daily 9am–10pm; Oct–end Mar daily 9–4.30 💷 Free; donations welcomed

Kirkwall and St. Magnus Cathedral

Kirkwall is the largest town in Orkney and the island capital. St. Magnus Cathedral, founded in 1137 and built over a period of 300 years, has architectural details from Norman to early Gothic. The exquisite carving, the red and yellow stone and its small size give it a feeling of delicacy and lightness for a medieval cathedral.

✚ 138 E2 ✉ Kirkwall

Maes Howe

This neolithic burial chamber is the finest chambered tomb in Western Europe. You creep through a long narrow stone tunnel to reach the central chamber. It was built 4,000 years ago with such precision that the sun lights the tunnel at sunset on midwinter. No treasures were found inside: Vikings had beaten the Victorians to the plunder.

✚ 138 E1 ✉ Stenness ☎ 01856 761606 ⏰ Apr–Sep daily 9.30–5; Oct–Mar Mon–Sat 9.30–4.30, Sun 2–4.30. Tours only: timed ticketing, must be pre-booked 💷 Moderate 🍴 Café (£)

Skara Brae

Best places to see, ➤ 36–37.

a walk around Shetland, Mousa Island and Broch

Mousa is a small, uninhabited island to the east of Mainland Shetland, with an unrivalled example of a broch – the circular, fortified, drystone tower of the Iron Age. Abundant wildlife includes seals and storm petrels, eider ducks, waders and skuas, which swoop and dive everywhere, unworried by the approach of humans.

Turn right from the jetty and follow the path along the coast to your right until you come to the broch.

Built between 100BC and AD100, Mousa Broch, featured in the great Viking Sagas, remains almost intact. A narrow passage leads to an inner courtyard where the encircling massive stone wall bears in on you as you look up at the circle of sky 12m (39ft) above. Torches are supplied to climb the narrow, worn stairs in the dark space within the walls. At the top you can see where great beams would have supported the turf roof and view a coastline that the original builders would still recognize.

Follow the path around the coast from the broch or head inland with the remains of a house on your right.

The map you get from the boatman indicates areas to be avoided during the nesting season. Either way you will reach two sheltered bays on the east side where seals gather. There may be just two or three swimming or possibly a hundred or so in and out of the water.

From the bay follow the path back to the jetty and the small stone cottage that now serves as a shepherd's hut.

Distance 6km (4 miles)
Time 3 hours (including ferry)
Start/end point The pier at Leebitton Harbour, Sandwick ✚ 138 C3
Lunch There are no facilities on Mousa, so take a packed lunch

SKYE AND THE WESTERN ISLES

This group of islands contain some of the bleakest and most beautiful scenery in Scotland. From the majestic Cuillins of Skye through the flat waterlogged moors of North Uist and the rolling hills of Harris to the timeless charm of the smaller islands, Eigg, Muck, Rum, Canna, Barra and Eriskay, you could spend a lifetime exploring here. Walk the ancient paths and hill tracks, seek out secluded bays or visit prehistoric settlements and still there are further delights to uncover.

www.visitthehebrides.com

🛈 Western Isles Tourist Board, 26 Cromwell Street, Stornoway, Isle of Lewis ☎ 01851 703088

Callanish Stones, Isle of Lewis

Built over 4,000 years ago, and 1,000 years before the pyramids of Egypt, this is possibly the most spectacular and intact prehistoric site in Europe. Standing on a raised site, the stones are 4.5m (15ft) high and form the shape of a Celtic cross. The main part of the site is a circle of 13 stones with an avenue of 19 monoliths leading north.

✚ 134 B2 ✉ Callanish ☎ 01851 621422

⊕ Visitor centre Apr–end Sep Mon–Sat 10–6; Oct–end Mar
Wed–Sat 10–4. Stones always open ✋ Visitor centre inexpensive;
no charge to view stones 🍴 Café (£)

Lewis Loom Centre, Stornoway, Isle of Lewis

Harris tweed production is one of the mainstays of the
local economy in the Outer Hebrides and is still woven
by hand. The only place in the islands where the entire
production process can be seen is the Lewis Loom Centre
in Stornoway, where Ronnie Mackenzie has set up a small
museum and exhibition display. Ronnie will demonstrate
carding, spinning and warping, and explain about natural
and synthetic dyes. Then he'll weave some cloth, talk
about waulking the finished material and
answer questions. His shop stocks a wide
variety of Harris tweed clothing.

✚ 134 B3 ✉ Old Grainstore, 3 Bayhead Street,
Stornoway ☎ 01851 704500 ⊕ Apr–end Dec
Mon–Sat 9–6 ✋ Inexpensive

Raasay Outdoor Centre, Raasay

Raasay is the place for adventure sports.
This outdoor venue provides equipment
and instruction for a wide array of activities
including sailing, water-skiing, sailboarding,
mountain bicycling, walking and climbing.
Accommodation is in the house where
Dr. Samuel Johnstone (1709–84), a leading
journalist and literary figure, and his
biographer, James Boswell (1704–95),
lodged during their tour of the Hebrides.
The activities are open to day visitors, too.
www.raasayhouse.co.uk

✚ 134 D3 ✉ Raasay House, Inverarish ☎ 01478
660266 ⊕ Accommodation all year, activities
Easter–Oct ✋ Expensive

Skye Museum of Island Life, Isle of Skye

This 'living museum' is a series of seven thatched black houses, reconstructed to form an ancient island township. The original black house on the site looks much as it did when it was last inhabited in the late 1950s. Here locals re-create the crofting way of life as it was a century ago. Behind the museum is the grave of Flora MacDonald who helped Bonnie Prince Charlie to escape the Hanoverian forces after his defeat at Culloden.

✚ 134 C3 ✉ Kilmuir, near Loch Ainort ☎ 01470 552206
🕐 Easter–mid-Oct Mon–Sat 9.30–5 🍴 Tea machine 💷 Inexpensive

ULLAPOOL

Ullapool, at the head of Loch Broom, was built as a planned fishing village in 1788 by the British Fisheries Society. Today, it is still a bustling fishing port, as well as the ferry terminal for the Western Isles and the main base for exploring Wester Ross. It has a lively venue at the Ceilidh Place, where people can enjoy the outdoors by day and sample live traditional music and dancing in the evening. The surrounding countryside abounds in walks such as the old drove road to Loch Achall and back over the summit of Meall Mor, with a breathtaking view over Loch Broom and the Summer Isles.

The Isles are a small group of uninhabited islands accessible by boat from Ullapool and Achiltibuie during the summer months. Most trips allow an hour on shore on Tanera Mhor, the largest island in the group. As well as sea birds, you are likely to see seals, dolphins and porpoises. Five kilometres (3 miles) from Ullapool on Loch Broom, you will find **Leckmelm Shrubbery and Arboretum,** dating from the 1870s, which is renowned for its rare trees and plants, including rhododendrons and azaleas.

Corrieshalloch Gorge, on the A835 south of Ullapool, is a 1.5km (1-mile) long, 60m (197ft) deep box canyon with an information board which tells you all about its geological and botanical interest. However, it is the Falls of Measach that most people come to see. The 45m (148ft) cascade can be viewed from a narrow suspension bridge that spans the gorge or from the observation platform.

✚ 135 C5

🛈 20 Argyle Street

☎ 01854 612135

🕐 Easter–Nov Mon–Fri 8–8, Sat 9–5.30, Sun 10–4

Leckmelm Shrubbery and Arboretum

✉ 5km (3 miles) south of Ullapool on A835

☎ No phone; www.gardensofscotland. org 🕐 Easter–end Sep daily 10–6

👋 Inexpensive

a drive around Harris and Lewis

This coastal drive around the islands of Lewis and Harris takes in the most important attractions in the Hebrides.

From Stornoway take the A859 towards Tarbert, which is 56km (35 miles) away on Harris. Continue on the A859 to Leverburgh. From Leverburgh continue on the A859 as far as Rodel, then follow the local road as it meanders along the east coast via Manish to rejoin the A859 south of Tarbert.

Called the Golden Highway, because of the expense of building it, this is a winding, single-lane road with passing places. It connects a number of small remote settlements strung out across a land that resembles a moonscape – rugged, rocky, empty and painfully beautiful.

From Tarbert drive back towards Stornoway on the A859. At Leurbost, turn left on the local road that links with the A858 at Achmore. Follow this road to Callanish.

The standing stones of Callanish (➤ 120), constructed about a thousand years before the pyramids, stand above Loch Roag.

Continue on the road past Carloway, Arnol and through Barvas to Lional, then follow the signs for the Butt of Lewis.

Carloway Broch is worth a visit, and the nearby village of Garenin with its restored black houses should not be missed. Arnol Black House was built in 1885 and served continuously as a dwelling until 1964. The young woman who lived there with her mother is now the caretaker and guide.

From the lighthouse at the Butt of Lewis return by the same route as far as Barvas then turn left on to the A857 to Stornoway.

Distance 298km (185 miles)
Time 6–8 hours depending on stops
Start/end point Stornoway ✚ 134 B3
Lunch Harris Hotel (££) ✉ Tarbert ☎ 01859 502154

Index

Acknowledgements

The Automobile Association would like to thank the following photographers, companies and picture libraries for their assistance in the preparation of this book.

Abbreviations for the picture credits are as follows: - (t) top; (b) bottom; (l) left; (r) right; (c) centre; (AA) AA World Travel Library.

4l Glenfinnan viaduct, AA/S Day; **4c** Glen Coe, AA/P Sharpe; **4r** Kilchurn Castle, AA/J Carnie; **5l** Cuillin Hills, AA/S Whitehorne; **5r** View from Calton Hill, AA/K Paterson; **6/7** Glenfinnan viaduct, AA/S Day; **11** Edinburgh festival, AA/ K Paterson; **12** Forth rail bridge, AA/J Smith; **13** Information Centre, AA/S Whitehorne; **14** Tour bus, AA/J Smith; **15** Taxi, AA/J Smith; **18** Policemen, AA/K Paterson; **20/1** Glen Coe, AA/P Sharpe; **22** Alloway, AA/S Anderson; **22/3** Kirk Alloway, AA/K Paterson; **24/5t** Burrell Collection, AA/S Whitehorne; **24/5b** Burrell Collection, AA/R Elliot; **25** Burrell Collection, AA/S Whitehorne; **26** Culloden Moor, AA/S Anderson; **26/7** Culloden Moor, AA/S Anderson; **28** Stained glass in St Margaret's Chapel, AA/J Smith; **28/9t** Edinburgh Castle, AA/D Corrance; **28/9b** Military Tatoo, AA/J Smith; **30** Glen Coe, AA/S Anderson; **30/1** Glen Coe, AA/S Anderson; **31** Piper, AA/S Anderson; **32t** New Lanark, AA/S Whitehorne; **32b** New Lanark, AA/M Taylor; **32/3** New Lanark, AA/S Gibson; **34** Rosslyn Chapel, AA/R Elliot; **34/5** Rosslyn Chapel, AA/M Alexander; **35t** Rosslyn Chapel, AA/M Alexander; **35b** Rosslyn Chapel, AA/M Alexander; **36/7** Skara Brae, AA/S Whitehorne; **37t** Skara Brae, AA/S Whitehorne; **37b** Skara Brae, AA/E Ellington; **38** The Tenement House, AA/S Gibson; **38/9t** The Tenement House, AA/S Gibson; **38/9b** The Tenement House, AA/S Gibson; **40** Traquair House, AA/K Paterson; **40/1t** Traquair House, AA/M Alexander; **40/1b** Traquair House, AA/S Anderson; **42/3** Kilchurn Castle, AA/J Carnie; **45** View from Scott monument, AA/J Smith; **46** Royal Yacht Brittania, AA/K Paterson; **46/7** View up Victoria Street from Grassmarket, AA/S Whitehorne; **47** View from Calton Hill, AA/R Elliot; **48** Museum of Scotland, AA/K Paterson; **48/9** Palace of Holyroodhouse, AA; **49** Palace of Holyroodhouse, AA/R Elliot; **50** The People's Story, AA/K Paterson; **51** Princes Street Gardens, AA/K Paterson; **52** The Canongate Building at the Scottish Parliament Complex in Edinburgh, Adam Elder/Scottish Parliament; **52/3** The Debating Chamber at the Scottish Parliament Complex in Edinburgh, Adam Elder/Scottish Parliament; **53t** Abbotsford House, AA/M Alexander; **53b** Abbotsford House, AA/J Beazley; **54/5t** Haddington, AA/J Beazley; **54/5b** Mary Queen of Scots House, AA/S Anderson; **55** Jedburgh Abbey, AA/S & O Mathews; **56/7** Kelso, AA/S &O Mathews; **58** Gladstone Court Museum, AA/M Taylor; **60** St Abbs, AA/M Alexander; **61** Culzean Estate, AA/K Paterson; **62** Museum of Modern Art, AA/S Whitehorne; **62/3** Glasgow School of Art, AA/M Alexander; **63** Charles Rennie Mackintosh, AA/S Gibson; **64t** Holmwood House, AA/S Whitehorne; **64b** Kelvingrove Museum, AA/S Whitehorne; **64/5** Kelvingrove Museum, AA/S Whitehorne; **65** Museum of Transport, AA/M Alexander; **67** The Tall Ship at Glasgow Harbour, The Tall Ship at Glasgow Harbour; **69** Templeton's Carpet Factory, AA/S Whitehorne; **70** Isle of Arran, AA/K Paterson; **70/1** Culzean Castle, AA/S Anderson; **72/3** Globe Inn, AA/M Alexander; **72/3** Dumfries, AA/P Sharpe; **73** Galloway Forest Park, AA/H Williams; **74/5** Wigtown, AA/J Beazley; **75** New Abbey, AA; **77** Sweetheart Abbey, AA/D Hardley; **78** Whisky, AA/J Smith; **79** Dee Valley, AA/R Weir; **80/1** The Discovery, AA/J Smith; **81** Frigate Unicorn, AA/J Smith; **82/3t** McManus Gallery, AA/S Day; **82/3b** McManus Gallery, AA/S Day; **83** Verdant Works, AA/J Smith; **84** Lower Largo, AA/M Taylor; **84/5** Loch Leven, AA/S Day; **86** Braemar, AA/R Weir; **87t** Bo'ness and Kinneal Railway Station, AA/M Alexander; **87b** Culross, AA/J Smith; **88** Crail AA/M Taylor; **88/9** Hill House, AA/K Paterson; **90t** Tobermory, AA; **90/1** Bullock, AA/J Carnie; **91** Inveraray, AA/S Whitehorne; **92/3** View from Ben Cruachan, AA/S Anderson; **94/5** Oban, AA/P Sharpe; **96** St Andrews, AA/J Smith; **96/7t** Pitlochry Highland Games, AA/S Day; **96/7b** St Andrews, AA/R Weir; **98/9t** Wallace Monument in Stirling, AA/S Whitehorne; **99** The Trossachs, AA/A Baker; **100** Haggis, AA/K Paterson; **101** Raasay from the Isle of Skye, AA/R Elliot; **102** Aberdeen harbour, AA/K Paterson; **103** Provost Skeen's House, AA/E Ellington; **104/5t** Ballater, AA/R Weir; **104/5b** Balmoral, AA/J Beazley; **106t** Bettyhill, AA/S Whitehorne; **106b** Cairngorms, AA/J Smith, **106/7** Neptune' Staircase, AA/S Day; **108/9t** Cromarty, AA/S Whitehorne; **108/9b** Fort William, AA/S Day; **110** Glen Affric, AA/J Henderson; **111** Inverewe Gardens, AA/J Beazley; **112/3** Loch Ness, AA/J Smith; **114/5** Lerwick, AA/E Ellington; **116** Italian Chapel, Orkney, AA/S Whitehorne; **117** Maes Howe, AA/S Whitehorne; **118/9** Grey seal, AA/M Moody; **120/1** Callanish Stones, AA/R Elliot; **122** Skye museum of Island Life, AA/S Whitehorne; **122/3** Ullapool, AA/S Whitehorne; **124** Butt of Lewis, AA/R Eames; **125** Carloway Broch, AA/S Whitehorne.

Every effort has been made to trace the copyright holders, and we apologise in advance for any accidental errors. We would be happy to apply the corrections in the following edition of this publication.

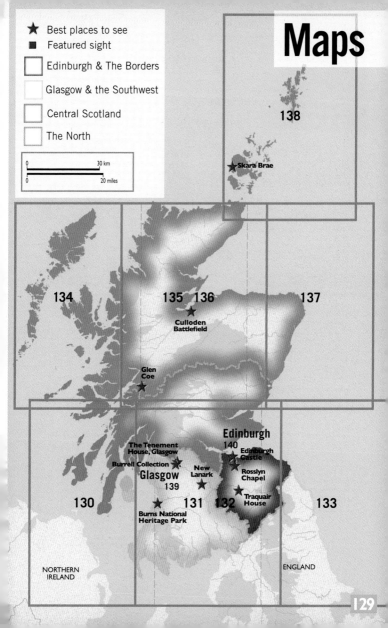

Maps

★ Best places to see
■ Featured sight

☐ Edinburgh & The Borders
☐ Glasgow & the Southwest
☐ Central Scotland
☐ The North

| 0 | | 30 km |
| 0 | 20 miles | |

138

★ Skara Brae

134 **135 136** **137**

★ Culloden Battlefield

★ Glen Coe

Edinburgh
140 ★ Edinburgh Castle

The Tenement House, Glasgow
Burrell Collection ★ ★ New Lanark
Glasgow
139 ★ Rosslyn Chapel

★ Burns National Heritage Park
130 ★ **131** **132** ★ Traquair House **133**

NORTHERN IRELAND

ENGLAND

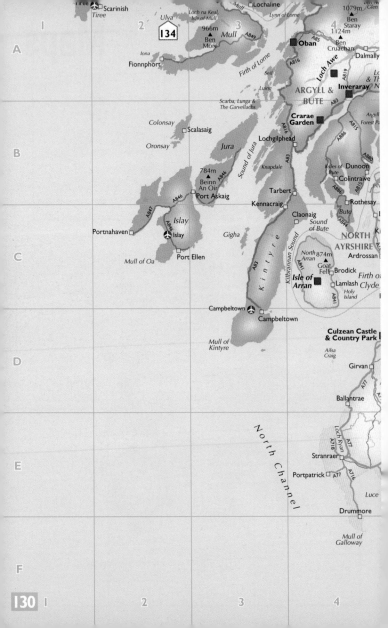

Tiree ⚓ Scarinish
Tiree

Ulva
Loch na Keal, Isle of Mull
Mull ⬜ Lochaline
966m
▲ Ben More

134

Mull
A849
Lynn of Lorne

1079m
Glen

4
Ben
Staray
1124m
▲
A85
■ Oban
Ben
Cruachan
Dalmally

Iona
Fionnphort
Firth of Lorne
Seil

Loch Awe

A816
A85
A819

Lo
& Th
N

Luing
Scarba, Lunga &
The Garvellachs

ARGYLL &
BUTE
■ Inveraray

Argyll
Forest Pa

Colonsay
□ Scalasaig
Lochgilphead ■
A83
■ Crarae
Garden

A815

Oronsay
Jura

Sound of Jura
Knapdale

A886
A88D

Isles of Dunoon
Bute

784m
▲
Beinn
An Oir
A846
Port Askaig

A83
Tarbert

Colintraive □

A815
A886
A815

Portnahaven □
A847
A846
Islay
⚓ Islay

Kennacraig □

Claonaig □

Rothesay
Bute

Gigha
Kilbrannan Sound
Sound
of Bute

NORTH

Mull of Oa
□ Port Ellen

Kintyre

North
Arran
874m
▲
Goat
Fell

AYRSHIRE
□ Ardrossan
□ Brodick

Firth
of
Clyde

Isle of
Arran
□ Lamlash
Holy
Island

Campbeltown ⚓
A841
□ Campbeltown

Culzean Castle
& Country Park

Mull of
Kintyre

Ailsa
Craig

Girvan □

North Channel

Ballantrae □

A77

Loch Ryan
A718
A77

Stranraer □
A75

Portpatrick □
A77
A716

Luce

Drummore □

Mull of
Galloway

1
2
3
4

Arbroath
rnoustie
Tay
rews Bay

Fife Ness
Crail
nstruther
enweem

Dunbar
A1
A107
St Abbs
Eyemouth
Berwick-upon-Tweed
mmermuir Hills
Duns A6105
A6112
A6105
Greenlaw
A698 Tweed
Coldstream
A6089
A698 Kelso
A598
rd
A698
Wooler
A697
Lindisfarne
(Holy Island)

Jedburgh
The Cheviot Hills
816m
The Cheviot
500m
A6088
A68
Northumberland
Coast

Shillhope
Law
Northumberland
National Park
Alnwick

Kielder
Castle
NORTHUMBERLAND
Otterburn
A1
Amble

Kielder
Water
Border
Forest Park
Bellingham
A68
North Tyne
A696
Morpeth
Ashington
A1068
A197
A189

Greenhead
A69
Tyne
Hexham
Corbridge A695
Gateshead
Bedlington
Blyth
A191
NEWCASTLE
UPON TYNE
Tynemouth
South Shields
TYNE & WEAR
A1

ton
A686
A68
A69
A691
Washington
SUNDERLAND
Consett
Chester-
le-Street
A690
A182
Seaham
A19

Alston
A689
Durham
A690
A177
Peterlee
A1(M)
A181

PENNINES
North
Pennines
893m
Cross
Fell
DURHAM
Crook
A690
Hartlepool
Bishop
Auckland
A689
A688
Stockton-on-
Tees
A19
A171

Appleby-in-
Westmorland
Tees
Newton
Aycliffe
A167
Redcar
Middlesbrough

Scotch Corner
Richmond
A6108
Catterick
A684
Northallerton
A172
A19
A171

133

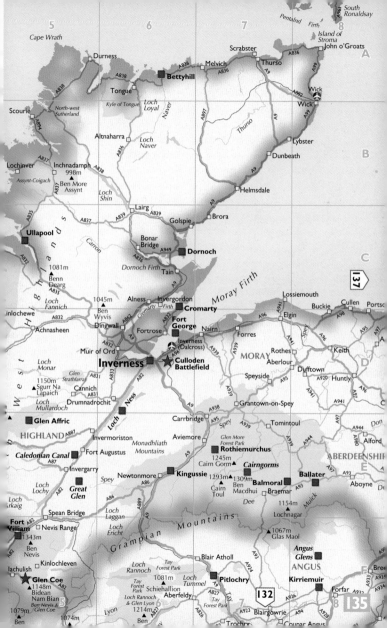

Pentalnd Firth
South Ronaldsay
Cape Wrath
Island of Stroma
John o'Groats
Durness
Scrabster
Melvich
Thurso
A836
A836
Bettyhill
A99
Tongue
Wick
Kyle of Tongue
Loch Loyal
Wick
A882
Scourie
North-west Sutherland
A9
Lybster
Altnaharra
Loch Naver
Thurso
Dunbeath
Lochinver
Inchnadamph
998m
Ben More Assynt
Loch Shin
Helmsdale
Assynt-Coigach
Lairg
A837
A839
Golspie
Brora
Ullapool
Carron
Bonar Bridge
A949
Dornoch
1081m
Benn Dearg
Dornoch Firth
Tain
Loch Fannich
1045m
Ben Wyvis
Alness
Invergordon
Cromarty Firth
Cromarty
Moray Firth
Lossiemouth
Buckie
Cullen
Portsc
inlochewe
Achnasheen
Dingwall
Fortrose
Fort George
Nairn
Forres
Elgin
MORAY
Rothes
Keith
Muir of Ord
Inverness (Dalcross)
Inverness
Culloden Battlefield
Aberlour
Dufftown
Huntly
Loch Monar
Glen Strathfarrar
A831
Speyside
A920
1150m
Sgurr Na Lapaich
Cannich
Loch Mullardoch
Drumnadrochit
Loch Ness
Grantown-on-Spey
Tomintoul
Alford
Glen Affric
HIGHLAND
Invermoriston
Carrbridge
Spey
Glen More Forest Park
Don
ABERDEENSHIR
Caledonian Canal
Fort Augustus
Monadhliath Mountains
Aviemore
Rothiemurchus
1245m
Cairn Gorm
Cairngorms
1293m
1309m
Ben Macdhui
Ballater
Aboyne
Invergarry
Newtonmore
Kingussie
Cairn Toul
Balmoral
Braemar
Great Glen
Loch Lochy
Spean Bridge
Loch Laggan
Dee
1154m
Lochnagar
rkaig
Loch Ericht
1067m
Glas Maol
Fort William
Nevis Range
1343m
Ben Nevis
Grampian Mountains
Angus Glens
ANGUS
Kinlochleven
Blair Atholl
A9
Kirriemuir
iachulish
Glen Coe
1148m
Bidean Nam Bian
Glen Coe
Loch Rannoch
Tay Forest Park
Loch Tummel
Pitlochry
Forfar
1079m
1074m
Schiehallion
Aberfeldy
Tay Forest Park
Loch Rannoch & Glen Lyon
1214m
Lyon
Tay
Blairgowrie
Trochry
Coupar Angus

137

132

135

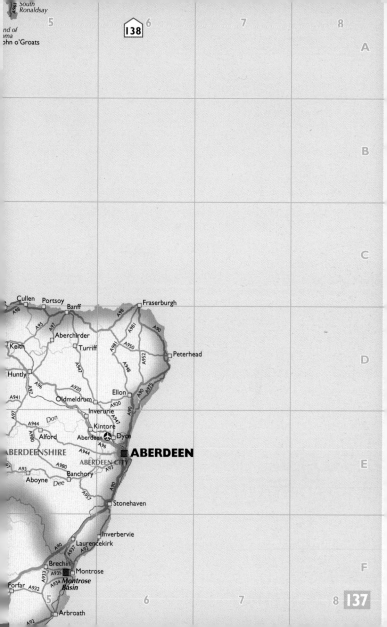

South
Ronaldsay

5 6 138 7 8

nd of
oma
ohn o'Groats

A

B

C

Cullen Portsoy
A98   Fraserburgh
Banff   A98
A95   A98
Aberchirder   A981
Keith   Turriff   A981 A950
A96   A948   A952
Huntly   Peterhead
A941   A90 A975
A96   A920   Ellon
A941 A97   Oldmeldrum   A920 A90
A944 Don   Inverurie   A947
Alford   Kintore   A90
A980   Aberdeen Dyce
ABERDEENSHIRE   A944   A96
A980   ABERDEEN CITY   ■ABERDEEN
A93   A93
A93   Banchory   A957
Aboyne   Dee   A90
A957
Stonehaven

D

E

Inverbervie
A90   Laurencekirk
A937
Brechin   A92
A933 A935   Montrose
Forfar A932 A934   Montrose
5 6   Basin   7   8
A90
Arbroath

F

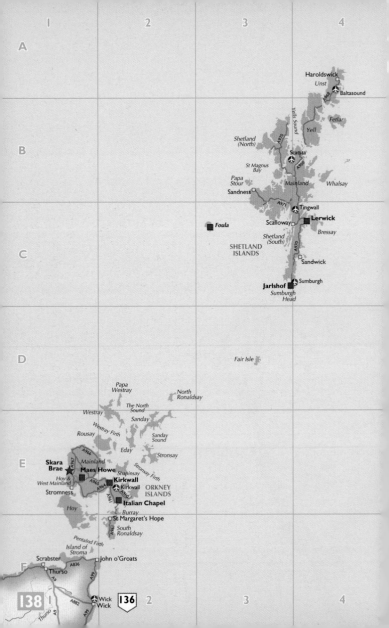

Haroldswick
Unst
Baltasound

*Shetland
(North)*

Scatsta

Yell Sound

Yell

Fetlar

*St Magnus
Bay*

*Papa
Stour*

Sandness

Mainland

Whalsay

Tingwall
Scalloway
Lerwick

Foula

*Shetland
(South)*

Bressay

**SHETLAND
ISLANDS**

Sandwick

Jarlshof Sumburgh

*Sumburgh
Head*

Fair Isle

*Papa
Westray*

*North
Ronaldsay*

*The North
Sound*

Westray

Sanday

Westray Firth

Rousay

*Sanday
Sound*

Eday

Stronsay

**Skara
Brae**

Maes Howe

Mainland

Shapinsay

Stronsay Firth

*Hoy &
West Mainland*

Kirkwall

Kirkwall

Stromness

**ORKNEY
ISLANDS**

Hoy

Italian Chapel

Burray

St Margaret's Hope

*South
Ronaldsay*

Pentland Firth

*Island of
Stroma*

Scrabster

John o'Groats

Thurso

Thurso

Wick

Wick

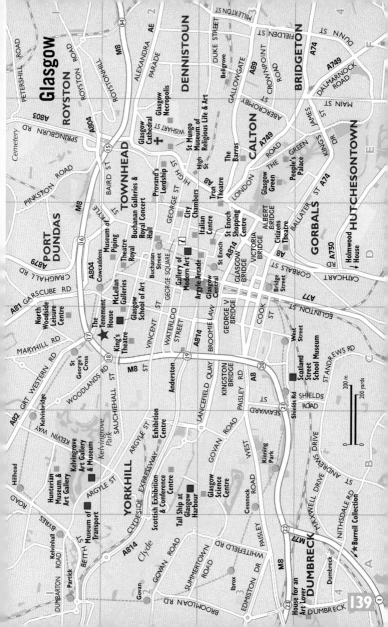

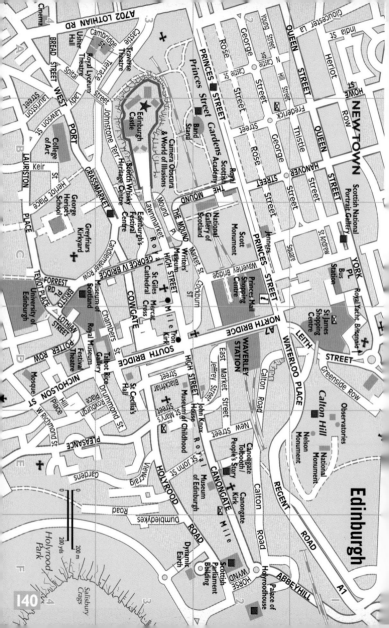

Notes

Notes

Notes

Notes